"Modern societ[...]e a woman. *Made* [...] by unpacking God's timeless design. With grace and humor, Kristen and Bethany challenge women to reject culture's push toward self-definition and instead draw their identity from the God who created them. Compelling. Readable. Re-latable. Bold. There's wisdom in these pages. So, grab some girlfriends and dig in!"

Mary A. Kassian, coauthor of *True Woman 101*, cofounder of the True Woman Conference, and regular guest on Revive Our Hearts

"This is a critical book for today, written by two women who are worthy of your trust. Kristen and Bethany bravely speak out biblical truth concerning gender, inviting us to shamelessly celebrate being female. They also stir up godly discernment and offer wisdom to navigate the confusion on one of today's most important topics. Every Christian woman and teen girl needs to read this book."

Dannah Gresh, founder of True Girl and cohost of Revive Our Hearts

"Though everyone is born of a woman, few today seem to know what a woman is. Because they stand squarely on Scripture, Kristen Clark and Bethany Beal have a ready an-swer. They unfold the beauty of biblical womanhood in this stirring book even as they offer a lovely mixture of honest reflection and cultural analysis as they go. *Made to Be She* is particularly good on the gospel that powers biblical woman-hood. Womanhood is not ultimately about a list of suggested behaviors; being a godly woman is about living out of the overflow of God's grace. It all starts there, and it all cycles back there: the atoning love of God shown in the cross of Jesus Christ. *Made to Be She* unfolds this vision and is a great resource for the rising generation today."

Dr. Owen Strachan, author of *Reenchanting Humanity* and *The War on Men* and host of the *Grace & Truth* podcast

"*Made to Be She* is a crucial message for women across the world. Understanding God's design for male and female changes everything. This book makes no apologies for its bold stand on biblical truth. It takes women on a journey of discovering their identity in Christ and helps dissolve the gender confusion that is so pervasive in our culture today. This is a must-read for every Christian woman desiring to better understand the beauty and uniqueness of womanhood."

Elizabeth Parsons, wife, mom of six, and founder of Purely Parsons

"Our culture struggles to even come up with a definition for *woman*, let alone agree on one! *Made to Be She* takes us back to our origin story found in Genesis and invites us to embrace God's timeless design for womanhood. Every woman needs to know that God made her to be she—both on purpose and for a good purpose. This book is a must-read for every Christian woman who wants to reject the lies and live out the truth of her femininity."

Shannon Popkin, author of *Shaped by God's Promises* and *Comparison Girl* and host of the *Live Like It's True* podcast

"We're living in a generation of people who can't even define the simple words *man* and *woman*. Enough is enough with this denial of reality. I love how Kristen and Bethany don't mince words in *Made to Be She*. They go straight to the source of truth and show us what God has to say about sex and gender. It's not confusing. Grab a copy. You won't be disappointed!"

Morgan Olliges, cohost of the *Paul and Morgan Show* and *24HRS WITH* on YouTube

"There are a lot of things promising us answers in our world today. As humans, we want to hold on to 'identity markers' that solidify our existence on this earth. The lie that we are facing today is that we are anything other than the beautiful design of an intentional and almighty God. *Made to Be She* takes us on a journey of rediscovering His good plan for our lives in how He created us. His loving plan helps us to thrive and flourish in His goodness. This is a must-read book for any woman who desires to truly know who she is and what it means to be a woman of God."

Addie Overla, host of *Christ in Me* podcast

"*Made to Be She* is the book this generation of Christian women needs. Femininity and womanhood have been all but eradicated by society in the name of progress and liberation. In this world of gender confusion and living out your own truth, we need to be reminded that God's truths still stand, that being a godly woman is a good thing, and that the 'advances' of feminism and new-age thinking are really getting us nowhere. This book is more than a guidebook to biblical womanhood. It's an all-out exposé on the thinking and movements that have taken over the beauty and purpose of being a woman. Kristen and Bethany have combined biblical truth, hard facts, and personal observations to create a compelling and informative must-read for Christian women everywhere."

Molly Maller, longtime active member of the Girl Defined Ministries sisterhood

Made
to Be
SHE

Made to Be SHE

Reclaiming God's Plan for Fearless Femininity

KRISTEN CLARK AND BETHANY BEAL

BakerBooks

a division of Baker Publishing Group
Grand Rapids, Michigan

© 2024 by Kristen Clark and Bethany Beal

Published by Baker Books
a division of Baker Publishing Group
Grand Rapids, Michigan
BakerBooks.com

Printed in the United States of America

Library of Congress Cataloging-in-Publication Data
Names: Clark, Kristen, 1987– author. | Beal, Bethany, 1988– author.
Title: Made to be she : reclaiming God's plan for fearless femininity / Kristen Clark
  and Bethany Beal.
Description: Grand Rapids, Michigan : Baker Books, a division of Baker Publishing
  Group, 2024. | Includes bibliographical references.
Identifiers: LCCN 2024015768 | ISBN 9780801094736 (paperback) | ISBN
  9781540904492 (casebound) | ISBN 9781493447008 (ebook)
Subjects: LCSH: Christian women—Religious life. | Feminism—Religious aspects—
  Christianity. | Bible and feminism. | Women in the Bible.
Classification: LCC BS680.W7 C53 2024 | DDC 248.8/43—dc23/eng/20240605
LC record available at https://lccn.loc.gov/2024015768

Cover design by Laura Powell

Baker Publishing Group publications use paper produced from sustainable forestry practices and postconsumer waste whenever possible.

24 25 26 27 28 29 30   7 6 5 4 3 2 1

From Kristen:

To my daughter, Caroline Marie.
You are fearfully and wonderfully made.
May the love of your Creator
compel you to embrace the beauty
of His design for your womanhood.
I love you more than words can express.

From Bethany:

To my daughter, Audrey Lynn.
You are precious and beautiful.
May God's design for your femininity
give you strength and courage as you grow.
I love you.

CONTENTS

Part 1: Womanhood Gone Wrong

1 · Seduced by the *Cosmo* Girl   15

2 · The Ditch of Feminist Womanhood   30

3 · The Ditch of Religious Womanhood   55

Part 2: Gospel-Redeemed Womanhood

4 · When Being a Royal Isn't Enough   77

5 · Rejecting Weak and Wimpy Womanhood   96

6 · Made to Be He and She   112

7 · God's Radical Design for Marriage and Sex   135

Part 3: The Shaping of Modern Womanhood

8 · When *She* Decides to Become *He*   155

9 · Falling for the Birth Control Pill   170

10 · Trading In Motherhood for a Career   189

11 · Chasing Beauty at All Costs   211

Part 4: Reclaiming God's Timeless Design

12 · I'm a W.O.M.A.N.   231

13 · Living Out Fearless Femininity   242

Acknowledgments   255

Notes   257

Part 1

WOMANHOOD GONE WRONG

chapter 1

Seduced by the *Cosmo* Girl

A wave of curiosity and confusion washed over me. As a ten-year-old girl, I (Kristen) had never seen anything like this before.

"Bethany, come here!" I whispered loudly to my sister through the store aisle.

The two of us were out shopping with our mom at a local resale shop. Bargain hunting (i.e., treasure hunting) was one of our favorite activities to do during the long, hot Texas summer months.

Hurrying toward me with a questioning look, Bethany's eyes got wide as she glanced at the store shelf.

"What in the world?" she asked.

Lining one entire row of the women's shoe section were pairs of the most beautiful, luxurious, and fashionable high heels we had ever seen. They were stunning! But what made these shoes uniquely intriguing to us was their *size*. These women's shoes weren't your average size eight or nine . . . they were all size *fourteen*. We had never seen women's shoes this large and this gorgeous before! So we did what any ten- and eight-year-old girls would do—we tried them on. Each grabbing our favorite pair of high heels, we attempted to walk an imaginary runway in the back corner of the resale shop. Giggling and struggling to keep the large heels on, Bethany walked toward me and said, "I wonder who owned these shoes. And why would she give them all away?"

Overhearing our loud whispers and noticing our complete fascination with the shoes, one of the shop employees approached us. "I see you like those shoes," she said with a smirk.

"We've never seen high heels this big before," I responded while quickly putting my pair back on the shelf. "What kind of lady brought these in?"

"Well . . ." the employee said with her smirk growing larger. "A lady didn't bring these shoes in."

Noticing the wheels of confusion turning in our little brains, she answered our question before we could even ask it.

Leaning toward us with a hushed tone, she said, "A man brought these shoes in. He's the one who owned them. He's the type of man . . . who enjoys dressing like a woman."

"Oh," I said slowly, my eyes wide. Neither of us had ever heard of something like this before. *A man dressing like a woman? What does that even mean?* With a dozen questions swirling around in our minds, we both slowly walked away.

The year was 1997, and this was our first exposure to cross-dressing.

A Radical New World

The past few decades have brought a tidal wave of radical changes to our modern society's perspective on sexuality, gender, manhood, and womanhood. What used to be considered a biological fact no longer exists. *What does it mean to be a woman? What does it mean to be a man?* These simple and straightforward questions have now become so complicated that even the most highly educated in our society cannot answer them. Lipstick, high heels, and a shaved beard can now turn any male into a female. In the name of inclusion, we're told to applaud the fact that—for the first time in history— a biological male (now a trans woman) received *Glamour* magazine's Woman of the Year award.[1] We're told to dismantle gender stereotypes by encouraging young children to watch grown men twerk while wearing fake breasts and provocative clothing.[2] We're told to "calm down" as we witness record-breaking numbers of teen girls (with no prior history of gender dysphoria) getting breast removal surgery because they chose to transition.[3] We're told to celebrate the progress as our nation rewrites the very definition of marriage itself.[4]

We've come a long way since 1997.

As we survey the landscape of our society today, it's hard to imagine that only a few short years ago, gender was considered a clear and uncomplicated concept by most people. Boys grew up to be men, and girls grew up to be women. The general public wasn't confused about this. Even the vast majority of liberals and conservatives agreed that marriage was between one man and one woman.

Thinking back on our own childhoods (and we're not *that* old), we remember being constantly affirmed in our biological sex and never wondered if there was a mistake. Even though I (Bethany) was a total tomboy, I was never asked by adults if I felt "uncomfortable" as a girl. I was never exposed to an endless buffet of sexual identities and gender options. Without the existence of social media and smartphones, we were encouraged to play outside and get our hands dirty in the mud. Life wasn't perfect and the world wasn't a utopia, but things were simpler, and most people agreed on basic matters of gender and biology.

> Boys grew up to be *men*, and girls grew up to be *women*. The general public wasn't confused about this.

So, how did we get to where we are today? When did everything get so complicated and convoluted? It might feel like the changes were drastic and sudden . . . but they were not. The bold new world we live in today is the result of a long line of dominoes that have been falling for decades.

Out with the Old, in with the New

The 1960s and '70s tipped some major dominoes that would ultimately change the way women viewed *everything*. Under the banner of feminism, women everywhere were encouraged to throw out traditional ways of embracing womanhood in favor of a more progressive version of femininity.

American journalist and feminist activist Betty Friedan, a popular influencer in this movement at the time, played a key role in transforming the minds of American women. She believed that women were trapped at home in domestic prisons and needed to be set free in order to truly flourish.

An article on History.com states that "Betty Friedan—who later cofounded the National Organization for Women—argued that women were still relegated to unfulfilling roles in homemaking and child care."[5] In her famous book *The Feminine Mystique*, Friedan wrote,

> The feminist revolution had to be fought because women quite simply were stopped at a stage of evolution far short of their human capacity. "The domestic function of woman does not exhaust her powers," the Rev. Theodore Parker preached in Boston in 1853. "To make one half the human race consume its energies in the functions of housekeeper, wife and mother is a monstrous waste of the most precious material God ever made."[6]

Friedan pushed the idea that a woman's happiness and satisfaction could be found only within herself. She stated that "we [women] need and can trust no other authority than our own personal truth."[7]

Nothing was off the table as feminist activists and leaders alongside the sexual revolution challenged traditional ways of living. Marriage, motherhood, family, gender roles, sex—all of it was being turned upside down in the name of women's liberation and autonomy. Things like the birth control pill and abortion were touted as "must-haves" for women in order to level the playing field with men. After all, if men could have endless sex without facing the "consequences" (i.e., getting pregnant), then women should have that same freedom. Marching under the banner of *equality*, women everywhere were told that true happiness and fulfillment would come only when all gender roles, distinctions, and differences were erased. It was out with the old, in with the new!

Ditching the Bible as an outdated book with antiquated and narrow-minded views, feminism marched forward, re-defining womanhood on its own terms.

Seduced by the *Cosmo* Girl

For decades, millions of women (single and married) have been enticed by the glossy covers of *Cosmopolitan* magazine. Known for its edgy phrases and provocative cover models, *Cosmo* set out on a mission to convince women in the 1970s and '80s that hot sex and steamy nights were the pinnacle of liberated womanhood. After all, the glossy magazine covers with their gorgeous half-dressed models were hard to miss. The bold captions in hot-pink ink were like magnets to the eyes. Phrases like *The Hottest Sex Tips of All Time* and *The 10 Things Men Want in Bed* intrigued every woman (and teen girl) who happened to pass by. Innocent grocery shoppers who were simply grabbing a few ingredients for that night's dinner were lured in by the sexy promises of a more passionate and exciting life.

Things like marriage, abstinence, and modesty were out-dated and dull. Stories of "liberated women" living in New York City whose lives revolved around hot sex and one-night stands presented themselves as a welcome break from real-ity. Fantasies involving a secret night of passion with the hot man next door appeared dangerously inviting. Going out for a night on the town in stiletto heels and a minidress might unlock an evening of passionate sex in the arms of a handsome stranger. Real women have sex with no strings attached. Real women find satisfaction in a life of loveless lust. *Just look at the evidence*, the *Cosmo* Girl says. *Story after story shows real women enjoying this fantastical lifestyle. And you can too!*

The only teeny-tiny problem? Most of the stories in the magazine were completely fake. These anecdotal, sex-obsessed women did not exist.

Sue Ellen Browder, a freelance writer for *Cosmopolitan* at the time, revealed her part in the *Cosmo* propaganda. She said, "From the 1970s into the 1990s I worked first on staff, then as a freelance writer, for *Cosmopolitan* magazine, where many stories we concocted about women having all these exciting, 'fulfilling' sex lives were completely made up. *Cosmo*'s editor-in-chief, Helen Gurley Brown, even had a list of 'rules' on how to write for *Cosmo*, which included guidelines on how to fabricate anecdotes about women who were living this supposedly carefree *Cosmo* lifestyle."[8]

In Browder's book titled *Subverted: How I Helped the Sexual Revolution Hijack the Women's Movement*, she reveals even more:

> The Cosmo Girl was not a real person but a *persona*, a mask the single girl lonely and alone in the world could put on to turn herself into the object of a man's sexual fantasies. . . . We urged the lonely single woman to let go of her "guilt" (moral concerns) and to sleep with any man she pleased, even if he was married. . . . Written in the intimate tone of "big sister talking to little sister," our unspoken message was "don't think about any of this too deeply, my dear, or you may spot the deception. Just relax and have fun. Leave all that serious thinking to the old fuddy-duddies." . . .

We had only one on-staff "fact-checker," a young, single, black woman who doubled as a file clerk and occasionally looked up a statistic or two in the *World Almanac*. But we had no legitimate fact-checkers, because we had few facts to check.[9]

Cosmopolitan magazine had a mission and an agenda. And it was working. The minds of women were being radically changed. A 1979 *New York Times* article told us that between 1970 and 1978, the Census Bureau reported that the number of couples living together had doubled in just those eight years.[10] And, as Browder points out, "Such is the power of skillfully crafted propaganda to change people's attitudes and lives. Fiction had become reality."[11]

Linking arms with the sexual revolution, *Cosmo* magazine helped push the message of women's liberation forward.

With feminist ideology transforming the home and family, it didn't take long for the next few dominoes to fall. Ditching a biblical understanding of male and female altogether, homosexual relationships were normalized. Marriage itself was redefined by the US Supreme Court in 2015 in *Obergefell v. Hodges*. Then came the redefining of the human body itself. Biological sex was severed from gender identity. This would have huge implications.

Looking back over the past few decades, it becomes easier to see how we got where we are today. One domino at a time.

A Tale of Two Ditches

As our culture has shifted further and further away from a biblical understanding of family, gender, and morality, it has become more challenging for Christian women to stay grounded in the truths of God's Word. As the two of us have examined our own lives and talked to thousands of women through Girl Defined Ministries, one thing has become clear. Even though the vast majority of us desire to honor God and live according to His plan, we seem to get repeatedly stuck in one of two ditches.

We'll call the first one "the ditch of feminist womanhood."

I (Bethany) was at a coffee shop the other day when I saw a college girl working on her laptop. What caught my eye was the backside of her computer. Every inch was covered in brightly colored stickers. Squinting my eyes out of curiosity, I read the following aesthetically designed quotes:

> The future is female.
> Keep your laws out of my vagina.
> Feminist. Feminist. Feminist. Feminist.
> I will not go quietly back to the 1950s.
> My body, my choice.
> Angry women will change the world.

This college girl is a typical example of how feminist ideology has saturated the thinking of women today. It's the air we breathe. It's the way we think. It's what we believe.

Sadly, this type of mindset has seeped into many of our churches too. As Christian women, many of us have unknowingly built our perspectives of marriage, motherhood, and morality on this version of womanhood. We've unintentionally adopted certain aspects of feminist thinking without even realizing it. As a result, the way we're navigating womanhood isn't grounded in biblical truth. This is what happens when we fall into the ditch of feminist womanhood (we'll unpack that more in the next chapter).

The second place we get tripped up is in "the ditch of religious womanhood."

Yes, you read that correctly. It might not seem like "religion" would be a problem for Christian women, but ohhhh, it can be. In fact, it was the biggest pitfall for the two of us.

As young women, we both took an interest in the topics of womanhood, identity, gender, and sexuality. As the culture around us shifted further away from a biblical worldview in these areas, we became even more passionate about understanding what the Bible taught. Both being avid readers, we devoured books on biblical womanhood, godly femininity, and what it meant to walk in God's truth.

Without realizing it, though, we began drawing hard lines in order to define what biblical womanhood *was* and was *not*. After all, we were rebelling against the cultural narrative in order to fight for God's design, right? We had our own "we can do it" women's mantra. Although our pursuit of biblical womanhood was rooted in Scripture, our application went beyond that. We were adopting extrabiblical rules for womanhood, thinking we were gaining clarity and confidence. We began measuring our worth and identity on our performance, not on God's redemptive work.

The ditch of religious womanhood can take on many forms. Maybe you can relate to our struggle of adding your own extrabiblical rules to Scripture. Or maybe for you, it looks more like passionately upholding things like godly marriage and motherhood but having very little grace toward women who believe differently than you. Or maybe it takes on the form of claiming the name of Jesus and attending church on Sundays but ignoring God in every other aspect of your life. Or maybe you're getting tripped up by trying to follow the Bible "perfectly" while completely forgetting to rely on the grace and strength of the Holy Spirit. The ditch of religious womanhood traps us when our actions look the part but our heart isn't rooted in genuine worship of God.

As enticing as they are, the ditches of feminist womanhood and religious womanhood aren't working. They're not landing us in a better place.

A quick glance at the state of modern womanhood today will not reveal a flourishing picture of women. You would think that after decades of feminists fighting for women's rights and happiness, we would be the most thriving generation of all. But this is not the case. Instead, modern women are plagued with record-breaking amounts of anxiety, eating disorders, and divorces. One out of every ten women (between the ages of eighteen and thirty-nine) use anti-depressants.[12] Author Carrie Gress stated that "happiness metrics confirm that women are struggling: Suicides, depression, substance abuse, and sexually transmitted infections have all increased dramatically over the last five decades. Women aren't becoming happier, just more medicated. . . . Something is going very wrong for the modern woman, despite the steady uptick of feminist advances."[13]

Women are hurting. We are broken. We are lost. We are disillusioned. The ditches of feminist womanhood and religious womanhood have failed us. They cannot give us true identity and purpose. Why? Because both of these ditches

> A quick glance at the state of modern *womanhood* today will not reveal a flourishing picture of women.

have the same underlying problem—they are completely void of the *true gospel*.

It's time for us to ditch these false ditches once and for all. If we want more for our womanhood, then we have to get on the only path that offers us true identity, purpose, and freedom.

It's the path created for us by our Creator.

It's the path of *gospel-redeemed womanhood*.

Why We Wrote This Book

It's been a few decades since the two of us encountered those unusually large high-heeled shoes in that resale shop. At the time, our understanding of God's design for gender was minimal. But we knew something wasn't right about a man dressing like a woman. Deep down we knew this wasn't how God intended things to be.

Today we know that gender matters deeply to God because it reflects a bigger story about Him as our Creator and Savior (see Gen. 2; Eph. 5). Womanhood is not a socially constructed idea carried on by ancient traditions and cultural trends—it's a God-designed reality that He established from the beginning of time. Your identity as a female was given to you by your Creator. You were *made to be she*. As our culture continues to shift from one pendulum swing to the next, gospel-redeemed womanhood has remained timeless and true. This version of womanhood isn't rooted in personal achievement or self-empowerment but in the finished work of Jesus Christ on behalf of sinners. It's for every woman who knows she's broken and in need of the grace and forgiveness of her Savior. Her life isn't lived to advance her own agenda, but rather she lives in humble surrender to God's Word, fueled by a desire to worship Him in all she does. Loving God more deeply and glorifying God more fully are what motivate and propel the gospel-redeemed woman forward.

Our goal in writing this book is to help each one of us pursue a Christ-centered, gospel-redeemed understanding of femininity that threads the needle of embracing what the Bible teaches without adding our own culturally informed ideas to it. Our generation of Christian women has been lulled to sleep by the alluring lies of this modern age, and it's time to wake up and reclaim what has been lost. Mary Kassian, author and professor of women's studies at the Southern Baptist Seminary, boldly stated, "I'm praying that God is going to raise up a counterrevolution of women. Women who hold the knowledge of our times in one hand, and the truth, clarity, and charity of the Word of God in the other."[14]

We must tune out the voices of *Cosmo* magazine and feminist ideology in favor of the One Voice who truly knows who we are. As we say in our book *Girl Defined*, "God is [calling] women like you to courageously go against the grain of modern culture. Women who will set a new trend, think outside the box, and raise the bar for femininity. . . . Women who refuse to live for the applause of this world and instead live for the applause of their King."[15]

No matter your age, background, or season of life, this book is for *you*. It's for the sisterhood of Christian women who want more than empty ditches. For the woman who is tired of relying on her own strength and is ready to rely on her Savior.

Are you ready to reclaim God's plan for fearless femininity?

Let's link arms and pursue this *together*.

Chapter 1 Study Guide

"Womanhood is not a socially constructed idea carried on by ancient traditions and cultural trends—it's a God-designed reality that He established from the beginning of time."

1. As you think back on your life, what has been most influential in shaping your view of womanhood? (i.e., parents, church, magazines, movies, friends, pop culture, famous influencers, etc.)?

_____

_____

2. In one sentence, write down what you believe it means to be a woman: *I believe a woman is . . .*

_____

_____

3. We've all been seduced by the "*Cosmo* Girl" in one way or another. Check all the boxes that apply to you now (or have applied to you in the past):

☐ Being skinnier will make me happy.

☐ Going on a hot date will satisfy me.

☐ Being loved by a man will fill my aching heart.

☐ Staying fiercely independent is the key to female empowerment.

☐ Having sex outside of marriage is no big deal.

☐ Maintaining a successful career will prove my worth.

☐ Being prettier would add to my value.

☐ Flaunting my body in a sexual way will give me the affirmation and love I crave.

How many boxes did you check? What has influenced you to believe those things?

_____

_____

4. As a woman, what do you believe is the key to finding lasting happiness, value, and worth?

_____

_____

5. In what ways have you fallen into the ditch of feminist womanhood and/or the ditch of religious womanhood?

_____

_____

6. Name three things you're hoping to learn by reading this book:

a. _____

b. _____

c. _____

chapter 2

The Ditch of Feminist Womanhood

Beating the guys was our number one goal. This "friendly game of basketball" had turned into an intense battle of the sexes. We were determined to squash our male opponents.

The two of us (Kristen and Bethany) were in high school at the time, and basketball was our passion. With both of us being over six feet tall, the game seemed tailor-made for us. Playing on our varsity team (with our dad as head coach), we lived for weekend tournaments and took great pride in every trophy our victories brought home. Our team was good. Like, really good. We only lost a few games the entire season and went on to win the national championship (two years in a row).

So, when these hotheaded guy friends of ours challenged us to a game of two-on-two, we didn't flinch. With the sun shining overhead, we met at a nearby park to settle our debate once and for all. Who was better? The guys or the girls? Today would reveal the truth.

With quick moves and accurate shots, we took the lead right off the bat. The hours of team practices and driveway drills had paid off. Our lead continued to climb. The frustration and disbelief on their faces only fueled our energy and focus. After twenty minutes of pounding the pavement, we were within one basket of winning. Glancing at each other with a knowing look, we pulled out one of our favorite basketball moves of all time—*the give-and-go step-through*. Before the guys even knew what had happened—*swish*—our shot went in and we claimed the victory.

Staring at us with unbelieving looks, the guys slowly walked toward us to exchange high fives. "Umm . . . wow," one of our guy friends said slowly. "Didn't see that coming."

Trying hard to hold back our smirks, we told them "good game," then headed to grab some water. Beating the guys felt so good. Like, *sooo* good. We would have never said it out loud, but deep down inside, the two of us had inklings of that age-old kindergarten chant rising up within us: "Girls rule and boys drool."

Do Girls Rule and Boys Drool?

Most of us have our own "battle of the sexes" stories to tell. As girls, there's just something we love about beating the boys, right? From a young age, we feel the need to prove that our gender is the better one. It's them versus us. We're determined to win—no—to demolish them!

This "them versus us" sort of thinking isn't new to our time. Generations of women have been proudly singing along to popular songs like "Anything You Can Do (I Can Do Better)" and "These Boots Are Made for Walkin'." In fact, the battle of the sexes goes all the way back to Genesis, when Adam and Eve sinned and he immediately pointed the finger at her (Gen. 3:12). But in more recent history, this battle reached a fever pitch a few decades ago, during what historians call "the second wave of feminism" (we'll unpack the other waves later).[1]

> The battle of the sexes goes all the way back to *Genesis*, when Adam and Eve sinned and he immediately pointed the finger at her.

Even though second-wave feminism happened back in the 1960s, this particular wave of feminism is important to understand because it would prove to be one of the most radically transformative movements for how women would come to view men, marriage, and the family. Leading feminist activists called for women to open their eyes and see their oppression. It was time to fight against their true opponent.

And who was deemed the main culprit of women's suffering at the time? *Men.*

And more specifically, the *patriarchy.*

Kate Millett was "a brilliant, but deeply troubled graduate student [who] decided in 1970 that she had discovered the real problem for women through the ages of the *patriarchy* (from the Greek words *pater* for father, and *arche* for rule)," according to author, speaker, and social policy analyst Sharon James. James goes on to say, "In [Millett's] book, *Sexual*

Politics, she used the term to describe societies where men rule over women. She argued that the means by which men rule is the traditional heterosexual married family."[2]

Millett set out on a mission to destroy the patriarchy. She gathered together with other women and formed "consciousness-raising" groups. Since most women weren't aware of their deep hurt and anger toward men, these groups were formed to help women see "the truth." The women would gather around a large table and open the meetings with a back-and-forth recitation. The chairperson would begin:

> "Why are we here today?" she asked.
>
> "To make a revolution," they answered.
>
> "What kind of revolution?" she replied.
>
> "The Cultural Revolution," they chanted.
>
> "And how do we make a Cultural Revolution?" she demanded.
>
> "By destroying the American family!" they answered.
>
> "How do we destroy the family?" she came back.
>
> "By destroying the American Patriarch," they cried exuberantly.
>
> "And how do we destroy the American Patriarch?" she replied.
>
> "By taking away his power!"
>
> "How do we do that?"
>
> "By destroying monogamy!" they shouted.
>
> "How can we destroy monogamy?"
>
> "By promoting promiscuity, eroticism, prostitution, and homosexuality!" they resounded.[3]

Kate Millett, along with other feminists who were a part of these consciousness-raising gatherings, would eventually become a member of the National Organization of Women. James says, "The revolution they wanted was the end of 'men-rule.'"[4] And they would accomplish this by destroying traditional marriage, gender roles, morality, and the American family.

Millett and other zealous feminist activists were passionate about their beliefs, and they would not stop until they accomplished their goals.

Down with the Patriarchy

You might look at someone like Kate Millett and wonder how she got to such a dark and extreme place. Why was she so vehemently against men and the family? What made her so hostile toward all forms of male leadership? Her background and home life might shed some light on this.

Millett was raised in a family filled with pain and anger. Her father was an alcoholic who beat her, then abandoned the family when she was only fourteen. Millett saw firsthand how cruel and evil a man could be. She was not loved or cherished by her father. She was abused and abandoned.

This heartbreaking story is one that many women have experienced—then and now. It's twisted and awful. No wonder Millett felt the way she did toward male leadership. And it's no wonder thousands of other women felt the same way.

As we dig beneath the surface, we can see that many radical feminists were hurting women, experiencing true and genuine pain. Like Millett, many felt abandoned within their homes and forgotten within their society. In their grief, they believed the lie that the ultimate source of their brokenness and pain was rooted in *men*. They assumed that by destroying male leadership, they would bring an end to their pain.

But although men had caused many women much hurt, the real evil at play wasn't men—it was *sin*. Sin was the true source of their problems. And it's the true root of our problems today too.

Although second-wave feminists blamed many of women's problems on the patriarchy, fueling the battle of the sexes, the "gender wars" didn't originate in the 1960s and '70s. Like we said, they go all the way back to the garden of Eden.

In the beginning of time, things were perfect between the first man and the first woman. Genesis 1 and 2 show God's magnificent creation of the male and female. Adam and Eve were created to be equal in value and worth but were intentionally designed to have differing roles and functions. There was no sin yet, so their marriage and gender distinctions functioned in perfect harmony. No pain. No brokenness. No battling. But then Genesis 3 rolls around and something dark and evil enters the scene. *Sin.*

> Adam and Eve were created to be *equal* in value and worth but were intentionally designed to have differing roles and functions.

Eve believes Satan's alluring promises of becoming like God and eats the forbidden fruit. Then Adam takes some, and he willingly eats too (v. 6).

When confronted by God Himself, Adam and Eve both resort to playing the blame game. Adam responds to God by pointing the finger at Eve: "The woman whom you gave to be with me, she gave me fruit of the tree, and I ate" (v. 12).

Then Eve responds by pointing the finger at Satan: "The serpent deceived me, and I ate" (v. 13). Nobody takes ownership. Nobody admits their sin. The male-female relationship is forever devastated by sin. God then gives Adam and Eve gender-specific consequences that strike at the core of their design as male and female. For Eve, God says, "I will surely multiply your pain in childbearing; in pain you shall bring forth children. Your desire shall be contrary to your husband, but he shall rule over you" (v. 16). For Adam, God says, "Because you have listened to the voice of your wife and have eaten of the tree of which I commanded you, 'You shall not eat of it,' cursed is the ground because of you; in pain you shall eat of it all the days of your life" (v. 17).

Right then and there, the battle of the sexes is born.

As author and filmmaker Carolyn McCulley tells us in her book *Radical Womanhood*,

> The result of this momentous decision is the world we live in [today]—a world fueled by selfishness, pride, and anger that results in conflict, death, and decay. When Adam and Eve sinned, they forfeited life in the goodness of the garden of Eden. They traded unhindered fellowship with God for the curses of marital strife, painful childbirth, futile toil, death, and most [devastatingly], separation from God. They were the first ones to sin, but we are no different. Genesis 3 teaches us that women do have a problem. But it's not men. It's *sin*. Sin warps everything, including the good that God has designed in being a man or a woman.[5]

As a movement, feminism did tap into a real longing to relieve the pain of womanhood. Many women were being mistreated and sinned against. Sexism and abuse did exist.

"But though it [feminism] identified some valid issues," Nancy DeMoss Wolgemuth points out in *True Woman 101*, "it failed to address them from a biblical perspective. Instead, it encouraged women to adopt an 'us-them' mentality, play the blame game, get angry, and claim the right to 'do it my way!' It added fuel to the battle of the sexes by inciting women to retaliate and fight back against men."[6] Sin breeds more sin. And the spiral continues.

This is what Kate Millett and other feminist activists didn't understand. Though they intended to lead women toward freedom and wholeness, they were only adding to the pile of brokenness, hopelessness, and pain.

The Feminist in Me

I (Kristen) was hanging out with a group of young people a few months ago through a local ministry in my city. There was a mix of children and teens at this gathering, and I naturally gravitated toward the teen girls. While I was engaging in small talk with a few of the girls, one of them suddenly turned to me and asked, "Are you a feminist?"

Surprised by her question, I smiled and said, "Well . . . I guess it depends on what you mean by being a feminist."

Leaning back with a thoughtful look, she swirled her fingers in the dirt. After a few seconds of pondering, she looked up at me and said, "I'm a feminist."

"Yeah?" I asked, welcoming her to share more.

"Yeah." She went on. "I don't need a man, and I'm never going to need a man. I'm a strong woman, and I can do things on my own." Her tone was bold and sure. Clearly, she had thought about this before.

Stepping into this conversation, we talked back and forth for a while about all things feminism, womanhood, and God's design.

That day, my eyes were opened to the fact that feminism isn't a movement from the past but an idea that is very much alive in the hearts of young women today.

Whenever Bethany and I talk about feminism through Girl Defined Ministries, we get a mixed response from our community. Some women push back against us and say that feminism is fighting for nothing more than equality between men and women. Other women have said things like "Feminism simply wants to help women reach their full potential." And others have said, "Feminism supports the personal choices of each and every woman."

It's clear that feminism can mean different things to different people. But regardless of whether feminism means something mild or extreme to you, it's important that we understand the history of where its ideas came from. It does not have neutral roots. As Christian women, we need to be careful that we're not unknowingly adopting a worldly version of womanhood by blindly embracing certain aspects of feminism.

As Mary Kassian points out,

It's important to remember that feminism is, in fact, an "-ism." The "ism" indicates that we're talking about a particular philosophical theory, a doctrine, a system of principles and ideas. Feminism encompasses much more than the cultural phenomenon of the women's movement. Feminism is a distinct worldview with its own ideologies, values, and ways of thinking. It contains [some] truth, but it also contains some powerful and destructive lies. And in so doing, it strikes at the very image of God and at an important earthly picture He chose to display the redemptive story. At its core, feminist philosophy is antithetical to the gospel.[7]

As a movement, feminism was so successful in transforming foundational ideas about womanhood that we don't even see it at play today. The society we live in has been so completely transformed by feminist philosophy that we don't even recognize the change. Everything—from womanhood, manhood, gender roles, marriage, motherhood, sex, and success to purpose, identity, and God's sovereignty—has been redefined. Feminist ideology has become the air we breathe today. So, naturally, we're going to inhale some.

Sure, women like Kate Millett are no longer leading us in "consciousness-raising gatherings," but her ideas about male leadership, marriage, and family have completely saturated our modern culture. For many of us, our views of womanhood, men, and the family have been deeply impacted by Millett's ideas without us even realizing it. The ditch of feminist womanhood is one that entraps each one of us in some way or another. Whether it's your perspective of success, motherhood, morality, male leadership, gender roles, God's authority, or something else— you've probably stepped into the ditch. The two of us sure have. Our goal in taking this intentional look at feminism is to expose the underlying anti-God agenda woven throughout much of the movement while also giving you a chance to reflect on how feminist thinking has seeped into your

Feminist ideology has become the air we breathe today.

own life. We want to help you disentangle your worldview from feminist ideology and plant it firmly back on God's Word.

To help unpack some of the specific antibiblical ideologies of feminism, we're going to take a look at the six biggest ways this movement sought to redefine womanhood. Be on the lookout for any threads of thinking that have taken root in your own heart today. And as you do this, remember that each one of us, whether we've openly identified with feminism or not, needs the grace of God equally. This isn't an "us against them" battle. Romans 3:23 reminds us that "all have sinned and fall short of the glory of God." As Christian women, our posture toward feminism shouldn't be one of pride but of humble gratitude for the gift of redemption won for us through Christ's death and resurrection. We each desperately need the light of Christ to shine in our hearts (2 Cor. 4:6), the scalpel of God's Word to expose our sinful thoughts and intentions (Heb. 4:12–13), and the blood of Christ to cleanse us (2 Cor. 5:21).

As you read the rest of this chapter, ask the Lord to examine your own heart and motives and expose any areas that are not rooted in the gospel and grounded in His Word.

The Four Waves of Feminism

First-Wave Feminism: Late 19th to Early 20th Century
The first wave of feminism focused primarily on women's suffrage and other legal rights.

Second-Wave Feminism: 1960s to 1980s

This wave focused on a broader range of issues, including the push for abortion, redefining gender roles, minimizing marriage, devaluing motherhood, and embracing sexual autonomy.

Third-Wave Feminism: 1990s to Early 2000s

This wave shifted gears by promoting sexual "freedom" (i.e., promiscuity) for women (think "raunch culture") and fought hard for the total deconstruction of traditional gender norms.

Fourth-Wave Feminism: Late 2000s to Present Day

Activists in this wave use online platforms to fight for issues under the banner of inclusion and social justice, such as gay and transgender rights, the #MeToo movement, and many other causes.

The Six Biggest Ways Feminism Has Shaped Womanhood

Goodbye "We," Hello "Me"

On July 19, 1848, over three hundred women gathered in Seneca Falls, New York, to launch a campaign calling for the social, civil, and religious rights of women. Spearheaded by abolitionist Elizabeth Cady Stanton, this meeting became known as the Seneca Falls Convention, marking the start of first-wave feminism. Winning the vote for women (suffrage) is what first-wave feminism is best remembered for.

However, there is another fascinating—and largely unknown—side to this story.

As professor Nancy Pearcey explains in her book *The Toxic War on Masculinity*,

> Today most history books present the fight for women's right to vote as an example of how men oppressed women and kept them down. But that's not how people defined the debate at the time. It was framed not as men's vote versus women's vote, but as the *individual* vote versus the *household* vote. . . . When the issue of women's suffrage was first raised, most women actually opposed it—a fact that puzzles modern historians. Why did most women oppose women's suffrage? . . . It was because they understood clearly that universal suffrage implied a shift from the household to the individual as the basic unit of society. . . . Why were women so concerned about a shift from the family to the individual as the unit of society? Because it struck a blow to the concept of male responsibility. For if society accepted that a man voted as solely an individual, then it no longer held him morally responsible for representing the common good of the entire household.[8]

As modern women today, we have been taught to view women's suffrage solely through the lens of women's freedom and equality. But as we dig a little deeper and look through the cultural lens of that time, we see a conflict of interest between women who wanted the family unit to remain the pillar of society and women who saw independence and individualism as the only liberating path forward.

Regardless of which side you're on in the debate over women's suffrage, the main point here is to see how first-wave feminism brought about a huge shift in society's view and function of the family. Society moved away from a "we" mindset and embraced a "me" mindset.

Looking back, we can see the impact of this movement played out in how autonomy and individualism reign supreme in our culture. Marriages and families function less like one unified front and more like independent individuals living under one roof. When the "me" is elevated above the "we" in society, marriages and families will suffer.

The feminist ditch of individualism = Shifting society away from the *family unit* in favor of the *individual person*.

Move Over, Dude—I've Got This

The café culture of Paris was a favorite hangout spot for the woman who would soon become credited with the rise of second-wave feminism. Simone de Beauvoir was a French philosopher and the author of *The Second Sex*, a book that would radically transform ideas around gender roles. Sharon James unpacks de Beauvoir's thinking: "Women are the second sex, argued de Beauvoir, because they are always defined in relation to men (taking the name of their husbands on marriage), and exist for their good (caring for their husbands and children). For women, marriage is no better than slavery."[9]

During the 1950s and '60s, women were being fed a steady diet of feminism that blamed gender distinctions as the source of women's oppression. To feminists, equality meant erasing gender roles. They demanded equal outcomes in society, pushing for 50 percent of each profession to become female. They believed that women could not find true happiness until they leveled the playing field between themselves and men. This meant equalizing every role, job, and position within the family, workforce, and government. They demanded 50/50 in *everything*. According to James, de Beauvoir believed "that there can only be genuine relationships between men and women when the woman is self-sufficient economically."[10] De Beauvoir's beliefs were a direct assault on God's plan for meeting the family's need for provision and protection through the husband, as seen in Genesis 1–2 (we'll unpack more of that in chapter 6). Women everywhere began believing the lie that true equality was only possible by erasing all gender distinctions and roles.

Today, the influence of this thinking is evident every time we minimize God's design for gender roles (specifically within marriage, the home, and the church) and push against biblical distinctions for male and female.

The feminist ditch of equality = A woman's value and worth can only be found by achieving gender role sameness.

Breaking Free from the Prison of Homemaking

With women now questioning the legitimacy of their feminine gender roles, Betty Friedan stepped onto the scene. In *The Feminine Mystique*, she paints a sensationally shocking picture of the American suburban woman, coining her deep discontentment as "the problem that has no name."[11]

She opens her book by stating that "the problem lay buried, unspoken, for many years in the minds of American women. It was a strange stirring, a sense of dissatisfaction. . . . Each suburban wife struggled with it alone. As she made the beds, shopped for groceries . . . she was afraid to ask even of herself the silent question—'Is this all?'"[12]

Later in the book, Friedan defines the "problem that has no name" as the "voice within women that says: 'I want something more than my husband and my children and my home.'"[13] The impact of her book was monumental. Friedan wasn't describing the true feelings of how most women viewed their lives at the time, but rather she was striving to bring about a revolution in thinking. She tapped into a woman's natural tendency to push back against her husband's leadership, which is a direct result of sin's curse from Genesis 3. And it worked. Everyday homemakers were suddenly struck with the realization of their "domestic oppression." Happy and content wives were suddenly acutely aware of their deep marital dissatisfaction. Women all across America bought into Friedan's radical messaging, believing the lie that happiness and fulfillment could only be found "out there."

Today, Friedan's ideologies on homemaking emerge every time a woman feels like the work she does inside her home (making dinners, caring for her family, cleaning, doing laundry, etc.) is far less important or purpose-filled than the work she could be doing *outside*.

The feminist ditch of homemaking = True female purpose and success can only be found outside the prison of homemaking.

Enter Marriage and Motherhood at Your Own Risk

As women were being awakened to their domestic oppression, the feminist movement pressed forward in its quest for liberation. This time, marriage and motherhood were on the chopping block. How could a woman reach true independence and freedom if she was trapped in the cage of marital and maternal duty? She must be freed.

Feminist Germaine Greer promoted the idea that marriage was the central way in which men kept women oppressed. In her book *The Female Eunuch*, she writes, "If women are to effect a significant amelioration in their condition, it seems obvious that they must refuse to marry. No worker can be required to sign on for life."[14]

Marriage wasn't the only hang-up for feminists, though. Activists had to figure out a way to overcome another huge obstacle: *biology*.

In 1970, a twenty-five-year-old feminist named Shulamith Firestone wrote the book *The Dialectic of Sex*, in which she argued that pregnancy was barbaric. Sharon James says of Firestone,

> She argued that nature had made men and women unequal, so that women through history had been forced to bear and rear children. Now scientific advances meant they could be liberated. The tyranny of the biological family could finally be broken. She argued that women *as a class* would be liberated by means of contraception, abortion, artificial reproductive technologies, and collective child-care. Firestone believed women would be happier if the embryo were placed in a cow or a machine.[15]

Firestone's disparaging views toward pregnancy and motherhood were taking root in the hearts of women. Just two years later (in 1972), the birth control pill became legal for all women (single and married). Then, one year after that (in 1973), abortion became legal in all fifty states. Feminist ideology had convinced women of the essential need for the pill and abortion by coining them as "fundamental rights" for female autonomy and liberation.

Today, feminism's degrading views toward motherhood and family are heard in the voice of every housewife who apologetically says, "I'm *just* a mom." Our society's low view of children is reflected in the fact that our modern homes are twice the size of what they used to be, but our family sizes have been cut in half. Our values have changed.

The feminist ditch of marriage and motherhood = True liberation is freedom from a "needy" husband and baby.

C'mon, Girls! Sexual Pleasure Awaits

Featuring braless women wearing wet T-shirts and engaging in provocative acts for the camera, raunchy TV shows like *Girls Gone Wild* set the stage for a new wave of feminism. As Carolyn McCulley says, "Third-wave feminists did an about-face, dismantling the opposition to pornography and sex work of the second wave by claiming participants in pornography and sex work can be 'empowered.' Raunchy had become synonymous with 'liberated.'"[16] Women were encouraged by radical feminists to flaunt their female power essentially by flaunting their breasts.

Melinda Gallagher, a sexuality professional, built a "sex empire" for women called the CAKE club. Wendy Shalit sheds light on these sex clubs in her book *Girls Gone Mild*. "Women paid to join, and were then able to purchase pornography and attend parties which resembled orgies."[17] Shalit also notes that "other leaders of third wave feminism equated 'dancing at strip clubs' with 'volunteering at a woman's shelter.' Both, they argued, could 'radicalize' women in a positive way."[18]

Sex was no longer attached to marriage or family in any significant way. With the pill and abortion secured, women could embrace hookup culture with a newfound freedom. Women everywhere believed the message that embracing an explicit and provocative lifestyle would not objectify them but empower them. Women were spurred on by popular feminist messaging from other women, like Gloria Steinem, who said, "A liberated woman is one who has sex before marriage and a job after."[19]

As women today, we accept this line of thinking every time we downplay the sacredness of marital sex in order to justify our immoral actions. When we minimize things like porn, erotica, premarital sex, and cohabitation, we're embracing our culture's philosophy for sexuality.

The feminist ditch of sexuality = Detaching sex from marriage will empower women.

I'm Not a Woman . . . I'm Just a "Person with a Period"

Recently, a female Supreme Court justice was asked the basic question, "Can you provide a definition for the word *woman*?" She replied, "I can't."[20] Welcome to fourth-wave feminism, where the very meaning of the word *woman* is in limbo. The first definition Merriam-Webster's online dictionary provides us is "an adult female person."[21]

In the name of inclusion and gender rights, the very meaning of womanhood itself is being erased. Numerous times, on various political commentary podcasts, in news stories, and so on, we've heard females referred to as "people with periods" and mothers referred to as "birthing people."

The modern idea that "anyone can become a woman" has thrown a wrench into the very "rights" feminism has sought to preserve. If anyone can become a woman, then who are feminists even fighting for anymore?

An article in *Teen Vogue* honoring International Women's Day stated that "womanhood is not defined by relationships, jobs, body parts, or anything else—it's not defined by anyone or anything but yourself."[22] Clearly, society has reached an all-time high in its confusion around gender and sexuality. Feminism no longer has an answer to the most fundamental and basic question of what it means to be a *woman*.

In our cultural climate today, it can be tempting for us, as Christian women, to accept the "inclusion" arguments and believe the lie that *womanhood* is a matter of choice rather than biology. And because it's so pervasive, it can be hard to even recognize when we do. With societal pressure boiling over, it can be tempting to go with the flow rather than standing firm on the truth of God's created order for gender.

The feminist ditch of modern womanhood = Women are being erased as men are welcomed into the fold.

Climbing out of the Ditch

As you can see, feminism is a powerful and intentional movement led by zealous women. Each wave was built on the one before it, bringing about radical changes that permanently transformed our society. But rather than women landing in a better place, we are more fractured and broken than before feminism began. "Women are less happy nowadays despite 40 years of feminism. Despite having more opportunities than ever before, they have a lower sense of well-being and life satisfaction."[23] Feminism isn't the answer to our longings as women.

When the two of us think back on our two-on-two basketball victory against the guys that day, we can see the subtle influence of feminist thinking in how we viewed our male opponents. Our drive to dominate the guys, put them in their place, and prove that we were superior was undoubtedly influenced by the culture around us. The battle of the sexes is still alive and well today.

I (Bethany) remember having to fight against a feminist mindset when I married my husband at age thirty. I had been thriving as a single woman for three decades, and now I had a permanent man in my life. I loved being married, but I had to fight against the mindset of individualism and autonomy. I still fight this mindset today.

I (Kristen) see the impact of feminism each day as I'm tempted to view the work I do inside my home (for my kids and my husband) as less valuable than "other work." In my heart, I know taking care of my family by meeting their daily needs is a beautiful way to glorify God (see Titus 2:3–5). But I have to regularly fight against the idea that true female success is only found "out there."

> Feminism has demanded the right to define the *self* and God, and in doing so, it has abandoned the *Creator* altogether.

As you read this chapter, did you spot any areas of feminist thinking in your own life? Which mindsets have you subtly bought into? How has your view of womanhood, family, and morality been shaped by feminism?

The ditch of feminist womanhood is large, and it entraps us all.

That's why it's crucial for us to remember that feminist womanhood isn't built on a biblical foundation but rather a worldly one. Its mantras are not rooted in God's Word. Its agendas are not in submission to God's authority. Feminism has demanded the right to define the self and God, and in doing so, it has abandoned the Creator altogether.

Yes, womanhood has been impacted and marred by *sin*. But turning away from our Maker is not the answer. If we want true redemption for our womanhood, we have to turn back to our Creator and Savior. We have to pursue a biblical framework for our womanhood. We have to spend time studying God's Word in order to value what He values and love what He loves. We are women, *made to be she*. Our female gender is an intentional part of God's design for humanity, with unique giftings, abilities, functions, and roles. God is calling us to embrace His design and to walk in obedience to Him. As Proverbs 3:7 exhorts us, "Be not wise in your own eyes; fear the Lord, and turn away from evil." We must choose to trust our Creator and believe that His design is for our good and His ultimate glory.

Gospel-redeemed womanhood is for sinners who are walking daily in the forgiveness and grace of Jesus, seeking not perfection but faithful obedience. It's the path for every woman who has tried doing things her own way, has felt the betrayal of sin, and is ready to embrace the way of her Creator.

Chapter 2 Study Guide

"Feminism has demanded the right to define the self and God, and in doing so, it has abandoned the Creator altogether."

1. Have you ever considered yourself to be a feminist (in the past or today)? If so, what did being a feminist mean to you?

_____

_____

2. After reading this chapter, has your view of feminism changed? If so, how?

_____

_____

3. How have you seen the "battle of the sexes" at play in your own heart and actions?

_____

_____

4. Check the box next to any of the six areas in which you've been influenced by feminist ideology:

☐ Independence and personal autonomy are essential to my womanhood.

☐ To be equal with men, I can't embrace any sort of gender roles or distinctions.

☐ I won't be successful unless I'm doing something important outside of the home.

☐ Marriage and motherhood are great, as long as I don't lose my freedom.

☐ Sex outside of marriage isn't that big a deal.

☐ If a man chooses to become a woman, why should I care, if it's what he wants?

5. Considering God's design for male and female, why is feminist thinking dangerous for a Christian woman to embrace (see Gen. 2; Eph. 5:22–33; Titus 2:1–10)?

6. What lies of feminism have you subtly bought into that you need to reject in your own thinking and heart?

7. Take a moment to pray Psalm 1 as a personal prayer back to God. Ask Him to help you grow and mature into a woman who truly delights in Him:

Psalm 1

Blessed is the man
     who walks not in the counsel of the wicked,
nor stands in the way of sinners,
     nor sits in the seat of scoffers;
but his delight is in the law of the LORD,
     and on his law he meditates day and night.

He is like a tree
    planted by streams of water
that yields its fruit in its season,
    and its leaf does not wither.
In all that he does, he prospers.
The wicked are not so,
    but are like chaff that the wind drives away.

Therefore the wicked will not stand in the judgment,
    nor sinners in the congregation of the righteous;
for the LORD knows the way of the righteous,
    but the way of the wicked will perish.

chapter 3

The Ditch of Religious Womanhood

(Bethany) walked into the jewelry store with one thing on my mind. I'd been dreaming of this day for as long as I could remember. Kristen had been wearing her purity ring for almost two years, and I wanted to join her in this step toward becoming a real Christian woman.

Wearing this purity ring would mark me as one of the "good" Christian girls. One who was committed to saving herself for her husband. One who would only date with marriage in mind. One who was saving her first kiss for her wedding day. And, of course, one who would get married in her early twenties and enjoy a lifetime of marital bliss.

Surely God would reward a good girl like me with a husband.

My purity commitments honestly seemed easy and reasonable at the young age of thirteen. Assuming I'd get married by twenty-one or twenty-two, I wouldn't be wearing this ring for very long. It was kind of a placeholder on my hand until the real thing could take over.

My dad and I browsed the store looking for *it*. My ring. I turned the corner and there it was. A stunning silver ring with little swirls encasing a dainty purple gem. *It's perfect*, I thought to myself. I pointed out the purple beauty to my dad and he agreed that it was the one.

My dad slipped the ring on my finger, and I felt like a grown-up for the very first time. A very young grown-up. But I was wearing a ring that marked my commitment to marriage. That was mature stuff.

The years rolled on, and I maintained my commitments. No sex before marriage. No casual dating. No kissing. No compromising the identity I found in being a "pure" Christian woman.

My early twenties were met with a series of unfortunate dating relationships. Despite my intentionality in dating, marriage just wasn't becoming a reality in my life. I had the purity ring. I had commitments. I just couldn't find the man.

The pressure to maintain my pure-girl reputation only increased as the years ticked on. I became known for my purity.

I was the good Christian woman.

I was the woman saving her first kiss for marriage.

I was doing all the right things.

This was my identity. This was who I was.

Mothers could point to me and tell their daughters, "This is what it means to be a godly Christian woman."

It's obvious now that I'd clearly fallen into a massive religious ditch and called it true Christian womanhood. The pride oozing from my life was almost palpable. Somehow

I'd convinced myself that I was saved by Jesus *because* of my commitments to purity. I was convinced that God looked down and expected me to obey certain rules in order to have worth as a woman.

Good actions equaled high value before God in my mind.

Don't get me wrong. Saving sex for marriage is a biblical mandate (see Gen. 2:24; Heb. 13:4). Having moral boundaries is in line with the wisdom found in Proverbs, Ephesians, and 1 Corinthians. Heck, even saving one's first kiss for marriage can be a wise boundary to better honor the Lord and the person you're dating. It's a matter of making sure the boundaries and convictions are rooted in biblical wisdom, a solid understanding of being saved by grace alone, and a heart that desires the Lord above the accolades of people. But in my late teens to early twenties, that wasn't the case for me.

You can imagine the devastation I experienced when a man I'd been intentionally courting crossed a few of my very black-and-white physical boundaries. We didn't have sex. We never even kissed. But he talked to me and touched me in ways I didn't want, and I was wrecked.

My feelings of worth plummeted. I was embarrassed. Ashamed. Disgraced. And I honestly questioned my identity as a Christian woman. My entire worth had been found in gaining the approval of others. I completely missed the fact that I was a sinner saved by the unmerited grace of God. "For by grace you have been saved through faith. And this is not your own doing; it is the gift of God, not a result of works, so that no one may boast" (Eph. 2:8–9).

My existence as a woman had been built on being able to boast about the good works I'd done and the way I'd followed

God's Word better than those around me. My foundation in life was "good works" and not "sinner saved by grace."

It's heartbreaking to write that, but it's the truth.

The ditch of religious purity culture had taken me too far. I was convinced I needed to earn my worth before God. I truly believed that my value was wrapped up in how good a Christian woman I could be.

The boundary-crossing relationship ended, and I was left to grapple with my worth before God. For the first time in my life, I took a deep dive into the word *grace* and strove to understand its true biblical meaning. I wanted to know how God viewed me. I wanted to understand what defined me as a Christian woman. Second Corinthians 12:9 was a big help to me. It says, "But he said to me, 'My grace is sufficient for you, for my power is made perfect in weakness.' Therefore I will boast all the more gladly of my weaknesses, so that the power of Christ may rest upon me." It's all about God's greatness and His power. I am worthy because of how great God is. I am loved because of how great God's love is (not because of how great I am). It's all about God. Not about me.

> I truly believed that my *value* was wrapped up in how *good* a Christian woman I could be.

The relationship and breakup also drove me to do a deep dive into what it means to be saved by God. I had been working to earn my salvation, but I needed to climb out of that ditch. Romans 5:8 helped me to do just that. It says, "But God shows his love for us in that while we were still sinners, Christ died for us." That little phrase, "while we were still sinners," changed me. While I was a sinner, Christ died for me. While I was imperfect, Jesus gave His life for me. He didn't save me because I was savable. He saved me out of pure love and grace and mercy. What a shift in perspective. What started out as a shame-filled dating encounter turned into the best spiritual journey of my life.

Her Roots Are Shallow

Women over the centuries have been falling into religious ditches and calling it true Christian womanhood. The lack of deep roots in Scripture and shallow relationship with Christ have driven us to live in anti-gospel ways. We've let everything *but* the gospel of Jesus define our womanhood.

From über-conservatism to flaming liberalism, Christian women have run the gamut of anti-gospel living. This book is about so much more than the war between conservative Christian women and feminist-minded women. There is a war going on between us as Christian women. Each group seems to think they've discovered "the way" to true godliness, and they look down on other women for not living like them.

Sadly, many of us are so deep in our religious ditches, we think we've found "the way," when in reality our roots are barely hitting the dirt. Take a minute to identify which ditch of religious womanhood you've been most prone to fall into:

Shallow Roots Lead to Ditches of Religious Womanhood

shallow roots → having a fundamentalist faith → doing good works to earn salvation shallow roots → having a liberal faith → twisting Scripture to support modern beliefs

shallow roots → having a legalistic faith → viewing Scripture through a list of dos and don'ts

shallow roots → having a pharisaical faith → measuring yourself against other people, not God

shallow roots → viewing Scripture as outdated and irrelevant → ditching your faith

What would you add to the religious path?

shallow roots → _____ → _____

Swept Up in the Movements

Most of us have been heavily influenced and shaped by the strongest Christian movements around us. Have you ever heard the saying, "Show me your three best friends today and I'll show you who you will be tomorrow"? It could also be said, "Show me the largest Christian movement of your day and I'll show you the kind of Christian woman you'll become tomorrow."

Having grown up in the 1990s and early 2000s, the two of us can see how heavily influenced we were by the purity culture movement. That was by far the strongest Christian movement sweeping the nation in our day. In an effort to combat the rampant STDs, AIDS crisis, and pregnancies out of wedlock, the purity culture movement made its mark. The two of us got swept up in the movement and devoured every

book and article written on the topic. Anyone else raised on
I Kissed Dating Goodbye?

The two of us desired to be godly Christian women, and
the purity culture megaphone was telling us that outward
perfection was the best way to achieve that. Unfortunately,
little was said about the heart in the reasoning for *why* one
should abstain from sex before marriage. The movement was
more about right actions than right heart motives.

Marshall Segal, author of *Not Yet Married* and managing
editor at DesiringGod.org, unpacks the ditch of religious
purity culture this way:

> Purity was not the final solution to AIDS, pornography, or
> teenage pregnancy; worship was. Purity wasn't the ultimate
> key to a better marriage or better sex; worship was. But teen-
> agers weren't angsty about worship; they were angsty about
> marriage, sex, pregnancy, and disease, so that's where the
> messaging often went (or at least what many kids came away
> with). Therefore, while teenage pregnancy and STDs did
> decline over the next couple decades (truly amazing when you
> think about it), many testified to experiencing more shame
> than freedom, more disillusionment than worship, more self
> than Jesus.[1]

We aren't the only ones who got swept up in a religious
movement. Women across the world have been and continue
to be caught up in compelling messages telling them where
to find their identity.

I (Kristen) was speaking at a girls' conference a few years
back. There was a girl at the event who stood out among
the rest. Her youth leader said this particular girl followed

the teachings in her church to the letter. She was an A-plus youth-group student. Whatever the leaders suggested the students do, she did. If they challenged her to share her faith, she did that. If they suggested the students court rather than date, she did that. She followed the loudest voices in her life and was held up as an exemplary student in the youth group.

This same girl grew up and ditched the faith of her youth. When she went off to college, the church near campus was very progressive. This young woman did what she had always done. She listened to the loudest voices in her life and aimed to be the exemplary member of what that church taught. Slowly but surely, the voices around her became more and more liberal, leading her to become an outspoken Christian feminist. She now spends her time fighting hard for things like trans rights and abortion on demand. For this young woman, the pendulum has swung from one side to the other. She's completely rejected biblical truth and has planted her feet firmly in the progressive Christian movement of her day.

I can't say for sure what happened to this young woman, but one thing is very clear. She never had deep roots to begin with (see Luke 8:4–15; 1 John 2:19). For whatever reason, her identity was found in living out the beliefs of the teachers, pastors, and leaders in her life. Her identity was all about being the best church member in whatever context she found herself.

I'm sure this young woman had no idea she jumped into the progressive Christian movement. It can be difficult to spot a movement when you're in the midst of it. It's much easier to look back and see the movements from an outside perspective. She probably assumed (like most people do) that she was on the right side of history and aligned with science.

Give it a few years and you'll be able to spot this progressive movement in the religious history books. That's why it's absolutely crucial that we, as Christian women, have a personal relationship with God and live for His glory alone. It's a must that every teaching we hear be filtered through Scripture and legitimately biblical—not just the opinions of people but the true teachings of God. If we neglect to do this, we will find ourselves getting swept away by the most popular and compelling religious movements (a.k.a. ditches) of our day.

A Look at Christianity and Womanhood over the Years

Let's jump back in time and look at some of the biggest Christian movements that have shaped women over the past few decades. We'll start back in the 1970s and work up to the movements of our day. See if you can spot any of the religious ditches Christian women fell into.

Egalitarianism Gives Christian Women More Power

In an effort to erase any discrimination or inequality between the sexes, the 1980s brought us Christians for Biblical Equality,[2] as well as Christian egalitarianism. Women had been homebound, barefoot, and powerless for far too long. The pioneers of the Christian egalitarian movement set out to free them from their so-called religious cages. Women no longer believed in the idea of being equal in value but created with a different purpose. In their eyes, any gender role differences meant diminished worth for women. They said that Christian women should not be excluded from any hierarchy within the home, church, or society. That all roles, responsibilities, and positions should be interchangeable between the sexes. Although Scripture clearly lays out unique roles for both men and women, husbands and wives, much of that was explained away in a desire to "even the playing field" in a Christian sort of way. Women began finding their identity in their newfound roles as pastors, elders, CEOs, teachers, and other positions of authority. Christian feminists began linking arms with secular feminists over a shared goal of equality.

The religious ditch of egalitarianism = Rejecting God's unique, non-interchangeable roles for men and women.

Conservative Organizations Emerge, Making Marriage and Motherhood the Goal for Women

A crucial meeting took place in 1988 that changed the course of the woman's role in society, church, and marriage. The founders of the Council on Biblical Manhood and Womanhood responded to the feminist influence that had crept into the church under the banner of Christian egalitarianism. This new council firmly believed that men and women were created by God to be equally valuable yet purposely different, a much-needed movement that helped bring clarity to the Christian church. The members at this meeting coined a term to clarify the Bible's teachings on the roles of manhood and womanhood: *complementarianism*. One of the founders describes the meaning of it this way: "Men are not superior to women. Women are not the 'second sex.' Men have a responsibility to exercise headship in their homes and church family, and Christ revolutionized the definition of what that means. Authority is not the right to rule—it's the responsibility to serve."[3] Within this line of teaching, men and women are viewed as having differing roles within the church, family, and society. Roles are not interchangeable. Again, this movement was much needed and has helped bring clarity and order to the home in a biblical way.

Unfortunately, several smaller groups and organizations took these much-needed biblical teachings and ran with them in an antibiblical way. Niche groups like Vision Forum, No Greater Joy Ministries, the Institute in Basic Life Principles, and many homeschool organizations of the 1990s emerged, taking these teachings to the extreme. These small organizations had a big impact on the thinking of conservative Christian women. They idolized the title of "wife and mother" (truly making it the pinnacle of womanhood). Sadly, the goal of womanhood became getting married and having babies. While marriage, motherhood, and roles within the home are good and biblical, the idolization of and obsession with them are not.

The religious ditch of conservative gender roles = Idolizing the role of wife and mom.

Purity Rings Become the Symbol of Godly Girlhood

No sex, no problems. At least, that was the hope of the purity culture movement. Beginning in the 1980s, we see a massive push among evangelicals challenging their youth to find their identity in abstaining from sex before marriage. What started out as a biblical teaching (sex being reserved for the marriage bed) turned into what some have called "the sexual purity prosperity gospel movement." Girls were often told that if they abstained, God would bless them with a husband and great sex. Which is false. God never promises us marriage or sex. He gives us guidance and instruction, but it's not for the purpose of getting the earthly life we want.

Over the next few decades, thousands of Christian teen girls got hooked on this movement and became obsessed with the purity pledge, wearing purity rings and other symbols of remaining a virgin until marriage.

While calling youth to save sex for marriage is good and biblical, it should not be something that youth find their identity in. The pledge of virginity became so trendy that female celebrities even got hooked and began showing off their purity rings. Honoring God and obeying the Word became an afterthought. It was all about reputation and ultimately getting the great guy and great sex as a reward for one's abstinence. Girls began to identify their worth and value by their level of "pureness" rather than by their identity as redeemed daughters of God. Obedience to God out of a love for His Word and a desire to do everything for His glory wasn't part of the picture. Shame was such a large part of this movement that many girls grew into women who are still struggling to reclaim a grace-based theology, and many women who ended up marrying are disillusioned by sex in marriage not being all they were told it would be.

The religious ditch of purity culture = Finding worth in living a "pure" lifestyle.

Megachurch Pastors Woo the Women

Fog machines, trendy cafés, charismatic pastors, and feel-good messages have lured modern women into booming megachurches. Many Christian women find themselves attending a local megachurch because of the superficial attractions and self-help messaging. Chris Brooks, the host of national Moody Radio's *Equipped with Chris Brooks*, describes the megachurch issue this way: "While the '90s gave us an unprecedented number of mega-churches, they also promoted a shallow, hyper-individualized faith culture that catered more to felt needs than to deep discipleship and spiritual formation."[4] Many women in these megachurch settings find themselves grappling for answers to the deepest questions about their identity and life purpose. We've heard story after story of women in these settings struggling with things like crippling anxiety and depression. Women might feel uplifted on Sunday morning, but they're left with empty answers to their real-life problems.

The religious ditch of modern megachurches = Little to no biblical discipleship on God's purpose for womanhood.

Women Trade Conservative Theology for Progressive Christianity

In the late twentieth and early twenty-first centuries, a group of progressive Christians emerged with new ideas of theological diversity, eclectic spirituality, and social-justice mantras. The progressive Christian woman views Jesus as a good teacher to admire and not so much a King to worship. Jesus is just one good teacher among many to choose from. Progressive Christian women are the first to champion female pastors, secular gender ideology, and a woman's right to end her pregnancy. This version of the faith is much more acceptable to our anti-Jesus society. The world doesn't mind a "Christian church" that holds to little biblical teaching. Progressive Christianity may seem to be a "more palatable version of the faith," according to Dr. Michael Kruger, president and professor at Reformed Theological Seminary.[5] Women have swung so far from the biblical teachings of Jesus that holding on to the title of Christian seems like a false representation of this belief system. Doing good and being a good person are a driving force for the progressive woman.

The religious ditch of progressive Christianity = Not truly worshiping Jesus as King.

Churchgoing Women Deconstruct and Leave the Faith

Who needs God when you can have total autonomy as a woman? Beginning in the late 2010s, many prominent female leaders began deconstructing their faith and moving away from Christianity altogether. Their influence created a movement of hundreds of thousands of women joining them in their departure. It's heartbreaking because many women leaving the faith have real religious hurts they're dealing with. Instead of confronting the wrong teachings, rejecting antibiblical viewpoints, and seeking true, compassionate, biblically based Christian counseling, these women have left the faith entirely. Many women who've deconstructed want nothing to do with their families or former Christian communities. The term *my truth* has become a gospel of sorts for the deconstructionist woman.

The religious ditch of deconstruction = Separating your womanhood from your Creator.

Getting out of the Religious Ditch

Religious movements have been leading women to religious ditches for decades. It's easy to look at some of the past movements and see how far they've strayed from true biblical teaching. I'm sure you've already spotted the religious movements your parents or friends grew up in or are a part of right now. It's easy to spot how other people have been caught up in something negative.

Think about it this way: You're sitting in church and you hear a really convicting message. Instead of self-examining, you think, *I wish so-and-so were here to get convicted by this; this is just what they need*, when in reality you should evaluate your own heart and look inward instead.

Take a minute to see if you can identify yourself in any of the six movements we just discussed. If you had to circle the movement that has most impacted your life up to this point, which would it be? In thinking of that specific movement, which religious ditch did that movement lead you toward? We're all influenced by the culture we live in, whether we realize it or not. That's why we need God's Word, to measure what we believe against what God says is true.

The two of us had no idea we grew up in the purity culture movement. We just thought we were godly girls doing things God's way. That's how religious movements often work. That's how women end up in religious ditches. That's how women begin looking to things rather than Christ to define them.

When I (Bethany) finally realized after that difficult breakup that I had been caught up in a movement, I made some drastic changes. I went to the Word for myself and took a deep dive into God's design for my life as a woman and for relationships. Passages like Hebrews 4:12 reminded me that the Word is the most important place to seek wisdom. It says, "For the word of God is living and active, sharper than any two-edged sword, piercing to the division of soul and of spirit, of joints and of marrow, and discerning the thoughts and intentions of the heart." I asked godly older women to disciple me so I could better and rightly understand the Word of God (see

Titus 2). I put myself under truly biblical teaching from a well-respected local pastor. I made sure I was under the teaching of that solid Bible-believing church to ensure I wouldn't swap one religious ditch for another. We see in Colossians 3:16 a call to live life with one another in this way. "Let the word of Christ dwell in you richly, teaching and admonishing one another in all wisdom, singing psalms and hymns and spiritual songs, with thankfulness in your hearts to God."

One of the biggest changes occurred when I stopped living my life to earn my worth before God. I stopped trying to maintain the reputation of the "good girl." I acknowledged that I could do nothing to add to or diminish my worth before God. And I changed the meaning of why I wore my purity ring. I didn't burn my ring or throw it away. I decided to use my ring as a reminder of God's faithfulness in my life, and I made it a symbol of my life verse on trusting God in every season:

> Trust in the LORD with all your heart,
>   and do not lean on your own understanding.
> In all your ways acknowledge him,
>   and he will make straight your paths. (Prov. 3:5–6)

You might think I was crazy for continuing to wear that ring, but it became a beautiful reminder of where I'd been in the past and where I was going in the future. It no longer represented a symbol of purity culture or my "good girl" status. It was a ring that reminded me to trust in God and worship Him more fully. I put that ring on a chain necklace and gave it to my husband as a wedding gift. It's one of the sweetest sights to see it hanging around his neck and to be reminded of God's kindness and grace in my life.

Slow down as you finish this chapter, and take time to consider your own story. How did you become the woman you are today? Which religious ditches have you been most prone to fall into?

Now consider how your life would look if you ditched your religious movements and grew deep roots in Christ. Deep roots in your identity as a redeemed daughter of God. You would no longer strive for the approval of others. You would no longer rely on your own "truth" to guide you. You wouldn't look to a relationship or a man to define you. Your identity would be found in the One who created you. You would dig into the Word out of a desire to know the Lord personally and seek His wisdom as your Creator.

Getting heavily involved in a solid church that both believes and teaches the Bible was life-changing for me, and I know it would be for you as well. Having the opportunity to live life-on-life with other Christians (in all seasons of life) is God's good design for us. The New Testament is filled with instructions on God's purpose for His people. We are not meant to walk alone in life or be exclusively a "podcast-listening Christian." It's so easy to be in the Word on our own but neglect showing up physically at church and inviting people into our life. We'll dig into this further in future chapters, but it's important to consider church with this topic of religious ditches.

Here's the kind of timeless biblical womanhood the two of us want to be a part of and are inviting you into as well:

deep roots → genuine love for God and an intimate
    relationship with your Savior → strong identity as a
    redeemed daughter of God

Sadly, this is light-years away from how most of us actually live on a day-to-day basis.

Most of us are living with our eyes half-closed, following the loudest voice around us. We're like spiritual deadweights wandering around, looking to someone or something to define us. We live earthly minded lives and look to momentary satisfaction to get us through the day: Grab a latte to boost the mood. Do what it takes to survive the workday. Hang with friends in the evening. Binge a show to wind down. Scroll social media to dull our anxiety. Fall asleep. Wake up. Do it all over again.

It's time to wake up and gain some clarity on your purpose as a Christian woman. It's time to gain some clarity on why God made you female. There has to be a greater purpose in God's design for women.

Chapter 3 Study Guide

"deep roots → genuine love for God and an intimate relationship with your Savior → strong identity as a redeemed daughter of God"

1. Shallow roots lead to religious ditches. Circle the religious ditch that you have fallen into or are currently in:

   Having a fundamentalist faith

   Having a liberal faith

   Having a legalistic faith

   Having a pharisaical faith

   Viewing Scripture as outdated and irrelevant

2. What causes a woman to have shallow roots in Christ?

   _____

   _____

3. Why is it crucial to have a biblical understanding of grace?

   _____

   _____

4. Look up Ephesians 2:8–9 and write down what these verses say about grace.

   _____

   _____

5. Review the section about deep roots and fill in the blanks:

deep roots → _____ → _____

6. Are you actively involved in a solid church that both believes and teaches the Bible (one that opens the Word and challenges you to be in it for yourself)? If not, what steps can you take to make church involvement (not just attendance) a part of your life?

_____

_____

7. Do you have a godly older woman mentoring you on a regular basis? If not, start praying about a woman you could ask to mentor you in the Word. Having godly input in your life is one of the best ways you can avoid falling into a religious ditch.

_____

_____

8. What was your biggest takeaway from this chapter?

_____

_____

Part 2
GOSPEL-REDEEMED WOMANHOOD

chapter 4

When Being a Royal Isn't Enough

She was an international icon. One of the most beloved women of all time. She landed herself on the cover of nearly every major fashion magazine in the world. She was adored, worshiped, and idolized. Women everywhere envied her luxurious lifestyle.

Diana Spencer skyrocketed to fame on July 29, 1981, when she exchanged her ordinary lifestyle for one of royalty. The wedding of Prince Charles and Diana Spencer has been described as a fairy-tale wedding and was watched by a global audience of over 750 million people, with over 600,000 adoring fans lining the streets, hoping to catch a glimpse of their new princess.

Princess Diana was everything the people of Britain hoped she would be. She was kind, gracious, compassionate, and seemed to connect with the people in a way no other royal ever had before. She was one of them. She got them. With all the adoration and worship any woman could ever hope for . . . something was missing. Princess Diana described her wedding with anything but joyful remarks. In 1995, in a now-controversial interview with Martin Bashir on BBC, she said, "The day I walked down the aisle at St. Paul's Cathedral, I felt that my personality was taken away from me, and I was taken over by the royal machine."[1] The heartbreaking remarks didn't stop there. Diana knew that fancy jewels, a royal crown, and stunning beauty weren't enough to satisfy. She went on to say, "I don't want expensive gifts; I don't want to be bought. I have everything I want. I just want someone to be there for me, to make me feel safe and secure."[2]

It only takes one simple internet search to see that Princess Diana was an incredibly lonely woman. She was surrounded by millions of adoring fans, but by all accounts, she was lost and lonesome on the inside.

Millions of people loved her . . . but no one really knew her.

Her entire identity became wrapped up in being a princess. Not just any princess, though. A princess who won the hearts of her people in a way no royal ever had before.

Tragically, Princess Diana lost her life in a car accident in 1997. She was only thirty-six years old. Many have blamed her death on the obsession of the people. Her life was under a constant microscope, and the paparazzi did whatever it took to capture glimpses and photos of the princess. Even to the point of car chases and compromising Diana's safety.

Shortly after her untimely death, she began to be called "the people's princess."[3]

Many have viewed that title as an honor reserved for the one they loved most, but I wonder if Princess Diana would have felt the same way. The very identity given to her is the one she most desperately wanted an escape from.

Diana's life story brings up some crucial questions. It challenges culture's assumptions about where happiness comes from, where lasting identity is found. Princess Diana had everything that we're told *should* make a woman satisfied, and yet she still felt incredibly lost and lonely. She had beauty, money, fame, adoration, servants, and literal royalty, yet it wasn't enough. It leaves us to wonder:

- How can having "everything" still leave a woman empty inside?
- If becoming a royal princess is every little girl's fantasy, why did Diana so desperately want to escape her life?
- If being a fashion icon and gracing the covers of every major magazine is the dream for women, why didn't it satisfy Diana?
- If being the dream woman of every man is so alluring, why did Diana feel unloved?

It's clear that having it all is not enough to satisfy a woman. Having the title "princess" isn't a strong enough identity to make one feel valued and loved. Living in a world where people line the streets just to catch a glimpse of you doesn't bring satisfaction.

Sadly, many of us, as Christian women, live our lives chasing these very same ambitions. We ignore the fact that having it all has never worked for any woman. Looking back through history, we can see over and over again that the biggest bombshell beauties of all time felt similarly to the way Diana felt. Take Marilyn Monroe, for example. (We unpack her story in our book *Girl Defined*. It's definitely worth reading, if you haven't already.)

Marilyn Monroe is still considered the world's sexiest blonde bombshell ever to exist. Take a walk in Hollywood, California, and you'll see that her image continues to be worshiped. Women often ignore the fact that she was deeply depressed and felt unloved and intensely alone. Her fame wasn't enough, and Marilyn chose to end her life in hopes of ending the pain. She was also only thirty-six years old.

Two bombshell beauties.

Two very different tragic endings.

Both at the young age of thirty-six.

It's time for us to take seriously the consequences of a misplaced identity. No amount of beauty, royalty, fame, sex, or wealth can ever satisfy. We need an identity beyond ourselves. We need something that will last.

Someday My Prince Will Come

Unlike Princess Diana and Marilyn Monroe, most of us aren't world-famous actresses or married to British royalty. We're not in line for a royal throne. We're not on the covers of popular magazines. We're not even on the cover of a small local magazine. For most of us, life is basic and ordinary.

So, where can we turn for answers? Where is a lasting identity found?

Feminist womanhood tells us identity is found in how we experience equality between the sexes and how similarly women are treated to men.

Religious womanhood tells us identity is found in being, doing, and believing the "right" things according to the church, our family, or the organization we're a part of.

But we know that both of those are dead-end ditches. No amount of gender equality or right behavior can give us a lasting identity that truly satisfies. I (Kristen) turned to the people of the internet to see if they had a better answer for me. I searched "How do you find your identity?" and this is some of what ordinary folks had to say:

> "Your 'identity' is simply the total of all the expectations and judgments you have about yourself for your life."

> "You can't find your identity, because it doesn't exist. Perhaps instead you should 'follow your bliss,' trusting your intuitions more, and notice what gives you energy."

> "You don't have a 'true identity,' but you do have an essential essence, and that is the really real you."[4]

Hmm, it seems the online world is struggling to define identity in any simple terms. I decided to take it a step further and turn to one of the most followed female celebrities of my day for answers. With her millions and millions of followers, I hoped she had something better to offer us as women.

Her answer to explaining her identity? "I am enough."

And you know what? Millions of other women think she's onto something. Those words have been repeated over and over and over again. Women have found some sort of comfort in reciting that phrase to themselves. *I am enough*. I've seen it printed on mugs, shirts, and bumper stickers. It's almost like if we say it enough, it will become true.

> No amount of gender equality or right behavior can give us a *lasting* identity that truly *satisfies.*

Being enough does sound amazing. But what does it actually mean? This widely recited phrase is what I like to call a fluffy, feel-good statement. It sounds beautiful and makes women feel good in the moment. But does it actually mean anything? Does it actually produce a real sense of identity?

It's clear that we need a lasting answer to this question. Without a secure source to turn to, we will always be left wondering, *Who am I, really, and what actually gives me value?* Instead of looking to other humans for the answer to this question, we're taking it deeper and going to the One who designed us.

From Five Husbands to Jesus Freak

There is story after story of women in the Bible who were radically saved by the grace of Jesus and came to understand their complete identity in Him. The Samaritan woman at the well is one of the prime examples of a woman who was saved by Jesus and embraced her new identity as a redeemed daughter of God. She wasn't just any woman, though. She was a wild woman, indeed. She had a long line of messy relationships and couldn't hold on to a man. I'm guessing she longed for unconditional love and went from marriage to marriage when she didn't find it.

Her scandalous reputation was well known, and other women did not associate with her. Her identity was marred by her sin. She was an outcast, forced into social solitude, so this serial divorcée found herself filling her water jars during the hottest hours of the day. That's when she encountered a man who would change everything.

Imagine her shock when this man approached her at the well and asked for a drink of water. A Jewish man approaching a Samaritan woman was unheard of in her day. This wasn't just any man approaching any woman, though. This was Jesus. The Messiah. The long-awaited Savior.

And Jesus knew exactly who she was. He knew who He was approaching, and He wanted to offer her a new identity in Him. He wanted to change the course of why she lived and what she lived for. He wanted to change her from a Samaritan woman to a daughter of the King.

Jesus and the Samaritan woman have a lengthy conversation at the well. You can read the entire story in John 4. It's actually quite fascinating. She is confronted by the fact that Jesus knows her past and the shameful details of her life. Instead of heaping shame onto this hurting woman, He extends love and mercy. He extends an invitation to become part of His family.

He pours His grace upon her.

He offers her new life in Him.

Redemption in Him.

New purpose in Him.

A chance to worship Him with all that she is.

He makes Himself known to her.

This outcast of a woman finds complete agape (self-sacrificing) love in Jesus. Overwhelmed with awe and wonder that Jesus pursued her and offered her salvation, she runs back to her village and begins telling anyone who will listen about the Messiah. God has chosen her. The long-anticipated Savior the people have been waiting for has come to her and offered her new life in Him. She has received a new identity from Jesus, and she is shouting it from the rooftops. Her faith cannot be silenced.

The woman at the well is overflowing with gratitude because Jesus went out of His way to pursue her and open her eyes to her need for a Savior. He showed himself to her, and her response was one of complete worship of Him. She goes on a missionary campaign and starts telling everyone in her village about the man who transformed her life. She is no longer the woman with five husbands. She has been forgiven, pursued, loved, and accepted by Jesus. Jesus ends up staying multiple days in her town, and a ton of people from her village accept Him as the one true Messiah. What's crazy is that we don't even know her name. We just know that she is the Samaritan woman at the well. That's the beauty of this story. She is not the main character. Jesus is. He is the Savior. He offers grace and mercy to the least of us. Knowing the woman's real name doesn't actually matter. Knowing her Savior's name is what it's all about. This woman went from searching for her identity in men and relationships to receiving her identity as God's child. She understood that *being saved by the grace of God* changes absolutely everything.

Here are a few other women from Scripture who were saved by God, and a beautiful faith emerged as a result. Each one of these women was given a new identity in Christ, and it changed everything about them.

Rahab, the former prostitute, comes to know the true God and risks her life to save His people. Knowing *Whose* she is gives her the boldness to put herself out there and live for something that actually matters. God's radical grace changed her heart and the course of her future.

Mary, the mother of Jesus, embraces the humiliation of being pregnant out of wedlock to bring the Savior into the world. Knowing *Whose* she is gives her the desire to embrace whatever calling God puts on her life. God's radical grace transformed her heart, and she desired to live as a servant of the Lord.

Mary Magdalene finds freedom from her demons and becomes one of the few women who travel with Jesus and His disciples. Knowing *Whose* she is gives her the power and freedom over her past of torment. God's radical grace was so evident in her life that she followed Him as a true disciple.

These women all had one thing in common: They were redeemed by the grace of God and lived in awe and wonder of their Savior. They each had a strong understanding of who they were in Christ. They knew Jesus had redeemed them and given them a new name as His royal daughter. Not because of how great they were but because of how merciful and gracious Jesus is. They were no longer defined by their bad actions or their good works. They were defined by God's love for them and His adoption of them into His family. This propelled these women of God to live courageous lives for their true King.

We can learn a lot from these women of Scripture. The centuries of separation between us don't diminish the similarities we actually share with them. Each one of them had a struggle with identity, and each one of them ultimately found hope and new life in God. His pursuit of these women and His unmerited grace in their lives is what changed them from the inside out. He showed them *Whose* they were, and that changed everything for them.

Stop Boosting Her Self-Esteem

The problem with many twenty-first-century women is that they don't see their need for Jesus. Most of us are pumped up daily with messages trying to boost our self-esteem and telling us how awesome we truly are. *You are worthy. You have what it takes. You're the queen. You go, girl! You are amazing. We believe in you. You are perfect. You're enough!*

This shallow messaging is actually keeping us from embracing our truest identity. Instead of filling our minds with shallow self-esteem messages, we need to recognize how lost and broken and empty we actually are. Just like the woman at the well. She came face-to-face with Jesus and chose to find true forgiveness and redemption in Him. She went from being a serial divorcée to a woman filled with faith in Jesus.

Finding your identity actually starts with honesty. It starts with acknowledging your inability to measure up to any standard of lasting worth. It starts with understanding that you're *not* "enough" and realizing that that's okay. You're not everything you need to be in this life, and that's okay . . .

because Jesus is. He came to be and do all that you could never be and do for yourself. He has shown Himself to you through His Word and invites you to accept true worth in Him.

When we come to Jesus with a repentant heart (acknowledging to God our sin and wrongdoing), we're acknowledging that we don't have what it takes and we need Him. We're actually doing the opposite of boosting our self-esteem and are instead coming to Jesus with the real, raw, broken, and dirty parts of our lives. We do this because we know He will offer us a new identity as His child (just like He did for the women in Scripture). Jon Bloom, cofounder of Desiring God and author of multiple books, says,

> If we come to Jesus with our sin desiring to repent, he says to us:
>
> - I will not condemn you, for I was condemned for you (John 8:10; 2 Cor. 5:21).
> - Come to me, and I will give you rest (Matt. 11:28).
> - I will love you forever and unfailingly (Ps. 103:17).
> - I will fill you with peace that surpasses understanding (Phil. 4:6–7).
> - And I will make you more secure than you have ever dreamed (Ps. 27:5; 40:2).
>
> There is an end to insecurity and all the fleshly striving it produces. It ends in Jesus. Let us bring all our insecurities to him and in exchange take his light burden of grace (Matt. 11:29–30).[5]

This is exactly what happened to the woman at the well. She was confronted with Jesus's love for her and realized that He wasn't condemning her for her past but offering grace and forgiveness for her to walk in. He was offering her everything that the men in her life could never give her. Love that truly satisfies.

Just as it was for her, repentance is your first step toward receiving your identity in Christ as His daughter. If you've never taken the time to get on your knees before God and lay your past before Him, do that now. Open your Bible to John 4 and allow Jesus's interaction with the woman at the well to guide you into your own time of repentance. Have peace going into this time knowing that Jesus died on the cross while you were a sinner and longs to have a personal relationship with you. He is full of grace and mercy. Titus 2:11 says, "For the grace of God has appeared, bringing salvation for all people." He wants you in His family as His daughter. John 1:12 offers us that invitation. It says, "But to all who did receive him, who believed in his name, he gave the right to become children of God."

Whose You Are Changes Everything

Once you understand your need for Jesus and have come before Him, saying, "I'm not enough, God. Please forgive me and be enough for me. Adopt me into Your royal family and give me a new identity as Your daughter," then you're ready to dig a little deeper into *Whose* you are as His redeemed woman.

Let's take a minute to dig into Scripture and unpack exactly how God describes your new identity in Him. Work through this slowly. This can change your life and the course of your purpose on this earth if you let it.

Gospel-Redeemed Identity

Here's a snapshot of what it looks like to receive your entire identity from Christ as a gospel-redeemed woman. Notice the order of how she builds her identity. Everything about her life starts with Christ and builds from there.

She is made in the image of God (Gen. 1:27).

She is a sinner in need of a Savior (Rom. 3:23).

She repents and seeks forgiveness (1 John 1:9).

She is no longer a slave to sin (Rom. 6:5–6).

She finds redemption in Him (Rom. 3:24).

She is made alive in Him (Eph. 2:5).

She is adopted as a child of God (Eph. 1:5).

She is sealed with the Holy Spirit (Eph. 1:13).

She is conformed to His image (Rom. 8:29).

She is free from condemnation (Rom. 8:1).

She is a part of the body of Christ (Rom. 12:5).

She has a heavenly inheritance (Eph. 1:11).

She is blessed with every spirit of blessing (Eph. 1:3).

She does everything for the glory of God (1 Cor. 10:31).

She worships the Lord (Ps. 29:2).

She lives as a servant of the Lord (Luke 1:38).

She fears the Lord (Prov. 31:30).

What a beautiful snapshot of the identity we receive when we put our faith in Jesus and accept His invitation into His family. The gospel-redeemed woman is so taken up with her Savior that she builds her life on a gospel foundation and lives in awe of her Redeemer. It starts and ends with Jesus. Her foundation is in Christ. Her heart is focused on worshiping God. Hebrews 12:28 casts that vision: "Therefore let us be grateful for receiving a kingdom that cannot be shaken, and thus let us offer to God acceptable worship, with reverence and awe." This is the kind of woman God is calling each one of us to become.

Imagine if you lived in awe of Jesus and His saving grace in your life. Imagine how radically different your mindset would be on a day-to-day basis. You wouldn't need to scramble for shallow accolades and temporary satisfaction. You wouldn't need a title like "feminist" to give you a sense of worth. You wouldn't need a bunch of religious rules to live by. You wouldn't need feminist ditches or religious ditches.

> When you truly believe that God has given you a new identity in Him and calls you *"daughter,"* it changes you from the inside out.

When you truly believe that God has given you a new identity in Him and calls you "daughter," it changes you from the inside out.

It's heartbreaking to think of women like Princess Diana and the loneliness she felt being surrounded by millions of fans but not really known by anyone. Imagine if she had fully understood the depths of God's love for her. His grace for her. We obviously can't speak with certainty about the condition of her heart, but it's sad to see how she spoke about her own life and the loneliness she felt. It makes us wonder how radically different her life would have looked if she had truly understood who her Maker was and had a deeply personal relationship with Him.

Knowing *Whose* you are should change *who* you are. And it should change what you live for. God doesn't give us a black-and-white map of exactly how we should live (He wants us to live by faith and reliance on Him), but He does lay out many virtues that He says are praiseworthy. Let's take a look at some of them.

Gospel-Redeemed Purpose

Here's a snapshot of some of the specific virtues God upholds as praiseworthy. These are from our book *Girl Defined*, which is definitely worth reading for more in-depth truth on your purpose as a woman. Notice how radically different these virtues are from virtues feminists hold up. God cares much more about the content of our hearts than the perfect actions we live out. These verses really speak to the kind of character this woman has.

She fears the Lord (Prov. 31:30).
She speaks words of wisdom (Prov. 31:26).
She welcomes hospitality (Prov. 31:20).
She teaches with kindness (Prov. 31:26).
She takes great care of her home and family (Prov. 31:27; Titus 2:5).
She loves and respects her husband (Prov. 31:11–12).
She loves her children (Titus 2:4).
She's not lazy or idle with her time (Prov. 31:27).
She works really hard morning until night (Prov. 31:15, 18).
She's respectful in her behavior (Titus 2:3).
She mentors younger women (Titus 2:4).
She's self-controlled in her words and actions (Titus 2:5).
She pursues purity in every area of her life (Titus 2:5).

God has a lot to say about womanhood. These verses make it clear that God-defined womanhood isn't measured by how much money we make, how many degrees we've earned, how prestigious our career, how big we've grown our ministry, how many kids we've had, how large our house, [how many followers we have,] or how fancy our car.[6]

God desires His daughters to be transformed by His love from the inside out and to live in line with their new identity in Him.

A Different Kind of Royalty

There are going to be loud voices screaming at you day and night, trying to tell you who you should be and what you should do. Telling you how you should identify in this world. Don't allow these ever-changing standards from society to get into your head. Don't allow the ditches of feminism or religion to define you. When you find yourself falling back into an old religious pattern or catch yourself being swept up by a compelling feminist message, come back to this chapter and use the Scripture passages above to help you refocus on truth.

And when all else fails and you find yourself struggling to be "enough," struggling with your self-worth, struggling to have a purpose worth living for, take time to do what you were ultimately made for: spending time in the Word and worshiping your King Jesus. This simple act will refocus your heart on the primary purpose for your existence. Jen Wilkin, a well-known Bible teacher and author, perfectly describes it this way: "Our primary problem as Christian women is not that we lack self-worth, not that we lack a sense of significance or purpose. It's that we lack awe. Awe helps us worry less about self-worth by turning our eyes first toward God, then toward others. It also helps establish our self-worth in the best possible way: we understand both our insignificance within creation and our significance to our Creator."[7] Yes, Jen. Yes. She nailed it. The answer to our identity isn't to look inward but to look upward and outward. To raise our eyes to Jesus and praise Him for His goodness.

A woman whose eyes have been opened to her need for Jesus is all about her King. Her identity has been transformed, and it changes her from the inside out. She lives in awe of the One who created her. You are a daughter of God. Not because of how great and worthy you are. But because of how great and worthy He is.

God's Word is timeless, and the verses you read above are relevant for you today and will be relevant for you in the future. They're relevant for the single woman, the married woman, the woman with kids, the woman without, the aunt, the widow, the grandma, and everything in between. Fifty years from now, your identity will still be found in Christ. Your purpose will remain the same: to know your Savior more deeply and worship Him more fully. It's really that simple. Knowing *Whose* you are will change everything about *who* you are.

Chapter 4 Study Guide

"A gospel-redeemed woman is so taken up with her Savior that she builds her life on a gospel foundation and lives in awe of her Redeemer."

1. How can having "everything" still leave a woman empty inside?

2. What were the two words used earlier in this chapter to describe how Princess Diana felt?

3. Which of the four women from Scripture most inspired you to find your identity in Christ? How did she inspire you?

4. Which of these descriptions of gospel-redeemed womanhood stood out to you the most, and why?

   She is made in the image of God (Gen. 1:27).

   She is a sinner in need of a Savior (Rom. 3:23).

   She repents and seeks forgiveness (1 John 1:9).

   She is no longer a slave to sin (Rom. 6:5–6).

   She finds redemption in Him (Rom. 3:24).

She is made alive in Him (Eph. 2:5).

She is adopted as a child of God (Eph. 1:5).

She is sealed with the Holy Spirit (Eph. 1:13).

She is conformed to His image (Rom. 8:29).

She is free from condemnation (Rom. 8:1).

She is a part of the body of Christ (Rom. 12:5).

She has a heavenly inheritance (Eph. 1:11).

She is blessed with every spirit of blessing (Eph. 1:3).

She does everything for the glory of God (1 Cor. 10:31).

She worships the Lord (Ps. 29:2).

She lives as a servant of the Lord (Luke 1:38).

She fears the Lord (Prov. 31:30).

5. Why does finding your identity in Christ matter so much?

chapter 5

Rejecting Weak and Wimpy Womanhood

Stepping off the plane, I (Kristen) couldn't believe I was actually in Italy. Zack and I had been married for less than a year and had the incredible opportunity to take this European trip with his family. Piling into a taxi van, the six of us made our way across Rome to our hotel. I couldn't believe my eyes as we drove past the well-intact ruins of the Roman Colosseum. We dumped our bags on the floor of our room and quickly made our way toward the city center to explore.

After grabbing some authentic Italian pizza and gelato (yes, it's better), we decided to do some shopping. Weaving our way through the crowds on the sidewalks, we passed dozens of street vendors who were trying to sell us every type of souvenir imaginable.

When we got to one street vendor, I squeezed Zack's hand to signal for him to stop. I couldn't believe what I was looking at. With a blanket sprawled out across the ground and music playing, this man was selling the most extraordinary toy. Right there in front of our eyes were dozens of little Mickey Mouse paper dolls dancing in the air without anything holding them. They were free-floating! I know. It sounds completely bizarre. But hear me out. This vendor had a large boom box playing music next to the paper dolls. He would pick up a new paper doll from his box, rub it on the speaker, then set it on the ground, and it would actually begin to *dance* by itself. With legs made of string! Not kidding.

Overcome by awe and curiosity, I whispered to Zack to ask the guy how he did it.

"How are they dancing on their own?" my husband asked with a questioning look.

"It's the sound waves that make them dance!" the vendor responded enthusiastically.

That's incredible, I thought. I had to have one—no *ten*! I would bring one back for each person in my family. This was the most incredible toy I had ever seen. A levitating, dancing paper doll!

Upon arriving back home in the US, I enthusiastically told my family about the unbelievable dancing Mickey dolls. I then pulled the ten-pack out of my bag to demonstrate the miracle for my curious audience. I turned on some music and stood in front of the speaker, ready to amaze them. Then, just like the street vendor, I rubbed my Mickey Mouse doll against the speaker and held it out to reveal the magic.

Drop. Mickey fell to the ground.

Hmm.

I tried again. More rubbing.

Drop.

Shocked and confused, I didn't know what to do. Why wasn't he dancing?

After a long and silent pause, my dad smiled and said, "I think you got shellacked."

Everyone laughed.

"But I saw it with my own eyes," I responded, feeling a bit less confident now.

A quick internet search revealed that I had indeed been shellacked. Big-time.

Video after video revealed the truth about the dancing-Mickey scheme. It wasn't magic. It wasn't music. It was a simple trick. How did the dolls dance in midair?

A hidden fishing string connected to the music player.

That was it. How could I have been so stupid?

I joined in the laughter as I threw my dumb paper dolls in the trash.

Weak and Wimpy Women

As Christian women today, we live in a world where dancing-Mickey schemes are everywhere. Not the paper-doll kind but the spiritually deceptive kind. Truth has been turned upside down. Wrong is now called right, and right is now called wrong. Things like personal identity, gender, marriage, family, and sex have been so radically redefined that we're struggling to know what's true anymore. From movies we watch to magazines we consume to social media accounts we follow, we're constantly bombarded with lies, deception, and crafty schemes that stand in complete opposition to

God's Word. Without even realizing it, many of us are being easily taken captive by these worldly philosophies because they appear so convincing.

Collectively, we are becoming a generation of spiritually weak and wimpy women. Our roots are shallow. Our faith is skin deep. Our understanding of God's Word is elementary. We are easily taken captive by unbiblical ideas that look spiritual but aren't rooted in truth. We're vulnerable to deception because our discernment has not been shaped by God's Word.

> *Truth* has been turned upside down. Wrong is now called right, and right is now called wrong.

Shallow theology leads to shallow roots. And that's exactly why we end up in *ditches*. The ditches of both feminist and religious womanhood are built on unbiblical ideologies. Second Timothy 3:6–7 warns women of this danger. "Among them are those who creep into households and capture *weak women*, burdened with sins and led astray by various passions, always learning and never able to arrive at a knowledge of the truth" (emphasis added).

The "creeps" who are capturing weak women can be represented by any person or lie that draws us away from God's truth. Just as Eve was lured away by the creeping snake who asked, "Did God *really* say not to do that?" (see Gen. 3:1), we are lured away by the same creepy lies from the same enemy.

Did God really say premarital sex is wrong?

Did God really say gender roles matter?

Did God really say marriage is between a man and a woman?

Did God really say being a part of a local church is important?

Did God really say divorce is a big deal?

Did God really say you shouldn't follow your heart?

These crafty lies creep into our lives and capture spiritually weak women. As 2 Timothy 3:6 points out, many of us are vulnerable to these lies because we're "burdened with sins and led astray by various passions." We're "always learning and never able to arrive at a knowledge of the truth" (v. 7). This means we don't have discernment because our lives are weighed down by lies and sin. We're always learning new spiritual insights but never growing in our understanding of biblical truth. Our desires and passions aren't bent toward the things of the Word but toward the things of this world. This is making us weak and wimpy women.

With more access to Bibles, churches, devotionals, women's studies, and spiritual apps than ever before, you'd think we would be the most spiritually robust generation of all. But we're not. We're easily deceived by dancing Mickeys as we follow what *looks right* instead of what *is right*.

There are many contributing factors to how spiritually weak we've become, but one of the biggest ones is this: We have become a generation of highly churched women who do not know how to read our own Bibles. We have become *biblically illiterate.*

This is a massive (yet silent) epidemic happening right now within our churches and Christian homes.

Jen Wilkin has noticed this problem for years. In response, she has become a passionate advocate for what she calls "Bible literacy." She says that one of the most severe problems for Christian women today is that they don't know *how* to read the Bible: "Many women spend their entire lives in church (even in organized studies), yet they are never taught even the most basic study methods. We exist on a teaching diet that's almost exclusively topical, yielding us a spot knowledge of Scripture at best. Bible illiteracy is rampant in our churches. Few of us possess foundational knowledge of our sacred text; even fewer know how to develop it."[1]

Ouch. It hurts to hear it . . . but she's right.

Bible illiteracy is a massive problem for us.

Instead of putting the hard work into learning how to study the Bible for ourselves, we go for the easy grabs through eye-catching devotionals and spiritualized self-help books. Instead of reading one complete book of the Bible to understand its context, we gravitate toward familiar passages and verses. We buy popular Christian books from the bestseller list, assuming they're theologically sound simply because we like the covers. We see aesthetically designed verses on social media and count that as our Bible time for the day. For the most part, our understanding of God's Word is stemming from secondhand teaching of the Bible.

We don't know it for ourselves. Therefore, we don't know what's *true*. We don't know what's right. We don't know how to cultivate and walk in a daily personal relationship with our Savior through the Word.

> We have become a *generation* of shallow Christian women who are easily taken *captive* by lies.

As a result, we have become a generation of shallow Christian women who are easily taken captive by lies.

Theologically Savvy Women

I (Bethany) was scrolling online through some of the most popular Christian women's books and devotionals the other day. The covers were beautiful. The titles were eye-catching. I could see why they were the most popular buys. But what stood out to me the most was how feelings-oriented they all seemed to be. Each title and design appealed to my emotions and feelings, making Christianity out to be nothing more than a self-help religion.

The titles felt more like self-esteem-boosting books encouraging me to feel better about who I am rather than exposing my sin and pointing me back to the hope of the gospel. These devotionals were focused on being positive and upbeat but seemed to lack true theological depth.

As women, we have been trained to accept "milk" as our main spiritual nourishment because that's what sells. We have become shallow in our theology because we're too intimidated to pursue spiritual meat. We often view theology as the stuffy subject for pastors or old men. This is a tragedy. Men (whether old or young) are not the only gender who should be studying the Bible deeply. In a fascinating article from The Gospel Coalition, it's noted that "not just men were given the first commandment to love the Lord with all their heart, soul, and mind [see Matt. 22:37]. God didn't make this calling gender-specific. All his followers love him in this way. Women need good theology, just as much as men do."[2] The word *theology* might feel like a daunting word, but it simply means the study of God. We as women need that too.

Studying the Bible in depth looks like approaching the Word with a desire to understand it intelligently. To study it academically. To navigate it systematically. Bible literacy requires treating the Bible with respect and intentionality. Just like you would any other book.

This is why being a member of a gospel-centered church that preaches the Bible faithfully is so important. Sadly, many churches today water down the Word by cherry-picking passages for a feel-good Sunday morning message. This type of preaching doesn't train us to be faithful women of the Word. My personal encouragement to you would be to find a church in your area that is committed to teaching the Word through expository preaching. This simply means that the Bible is taught in a systematic way (often working through one complete book from beginning to end), and the biblical text itself provides the main points for the sermon. This type of regular, faithful preaching will equip you to become a woman who knows how to study and apply the Word rightly.

Here's the amazing thing: As you consistently sit under faithful preaching and learn to pursue the Word with both your heart and your mind, God will use His Word in your life to mature you as a believer. You will no longer be a weak and vulnerable woman but a discerning and wisdom-filled woman. You will become fine-tuned to God's ways. Your discernment will grow as your roots are firmly planted in His truth. You will joyfully join the psalmist in saying, "Your word is a lamp to my feet and a light to my path" (Ps. 119:105).

You won't fall into ditches as easily because the path of truth will be well lit in front of you. You won't be weighed down by secret sins or trapped in worldly passions because your heart will be renewed by God's Word. You will be able to spot creeping lies before they have the chance to take you captive.

By studying God's Word for yourself, you will become a theologically savvy woman.

How to Study the Bible for Yourself

The sun was just beginning to peek over the beautiful hill country on this cool Texas morning. With my coffee in hand, I (Kristen) sat down on the couch to enjoy some much-needed time in the Word. Life had been full and a bit overwhelming lately. I was ready for this quiet moment. *Ahhhh*. It was going to be a lovely morning with just me and God. Setting my Bible on my lap, I tried to think of which passage to read. Going back and forth in my head, I decided to read John. *No . . . I just finished a Gospel book.* Maybe the Psalms? *No . . . I did that two months ago.* Staring down at my closed Bible, I suddenly felt overwhelmed by the sheer volume of it. *This book is so huge*, I thought. *What should I read?* Normally small decisions like this don't overwhelm me, but like I said, life had been full.

So I resorted to the only method I could think of in that moment. Closing my eyes, I laid my Bible on my lap, then blindly opened it and randomly dropped my finger onto the page. *Jeremiah 36. Well, there you go. I guess that's what I'm reading today!*

Okay, okay, I know that's lame. But let's be honest. Have you ever done that? I know I'm not alone in using the famous "close eyes and point" method. Thankfully, it didn't become my go-to Bible study method.

Like me, I'm guessing you've had your own moments of sitting down with your Bible, only to feel totally lost and unsure of what to do next. I get it. Knowing what to read, where to read, and how to read is a huge barrier for many of us.

Thankfully, we don't have to stay in that unsure state. You can effectively grow in your Bible literacy skills by learning some simple, yet powerful, methods for studying God's Word. Quite frankly, there are some less helpful ways and more helpful ways to approach the Bible. Learning how to approach the Word rightly will greatly impact your understanding and love of it.

Less Helpful Approach #1: The Bible Is a Book about Me

Sadly, many of the teachings in Christian churches today present the Bible as a book about *you*. You're encouraged to find yourself in every story and passage. You're told to insert yourself into everything you read. Yes, the Bible has plenty to say *to* you, but you are not the main character of this story. When you approach the Word with a "Where am I in this passage?" mentality, your Bible reading becomes a self-focused quest for inspirational motivation and little more.

Helpful Approach #1: The Bible Is a Book about God

The Bible was written to tell the story of *God*. He is the main character. From Genesis to Revelation, it's one long and compelling story of who God is and how He saved His people from sin through Jesus's death and resurrection. It concludes in Revelation with the hope of Jesus coming back again to make all things new. Instead of looking for yourself in every passage, look for God. Look for Jesus. Look for the gospel. This is the central theme of this beautiful story. When you do this, your heart will be drawn into awe-inspiring worship.

Less Helpful Approach #2: Hopping in and out of Passages

One of the most common ways people read the Bible is by jumping in and out of different passages every time they sit down. With short attention spans and microwave-fast mindsets, we don't stay in one place for very long. This method is a poor approach to understanding the full scope and context of Scripture. We will have a spotty knowledge of God at best.

Helpful Approach #2: Dig Into One Book at a Time

Rather than bouncing around like a lady stuck on a pogo stick, pick *one* book of the Bible and start reading that book from the beginning. This is how books are meant to be read. You would never pick up a new novel and jump right into the middle of it, so why do that with the books of the Bible? You will be much better served by starting at the beginning of a book and reading it all the way through from start to finish. By doing this, you will gain a deeper understanding of the book's theme, purpose, and intent.

Less Helpful Approach #3: Viewing Scripture as a Quick-Fix Reference Guide

We live in a society that leans heavily on the "pop a pill" mindset. This quick-fix mentality has translated into the way we approach the Bible too. We open our Bible when we need a quick fix. We're feeling down, so we "pop a Proverb" or "snag a Psalm." We grab a simple and encouraging verse to medicate our spiritual needs at that moment. But sadly, this approach often leads to applying Scripture out of context, leaving us with shallow application and short-term encouragement.

Helpful Approach #3: Studying Full Passages for Accurate Application

Context is king. Instead of grabbing a quick fix, you can find true healing and help by studying and applying the full passage as it was written. Instead of reading only a popular verse from Philippians, read the entire chapter (or even better, the full book) to understand what the author is driving at. This will help you understand how to apply well-known verses within the right context. It's also key to remember that we cannot invent personal application that the biblical author never intended for his original audience. Again, context is king.

Approaching the Word with intentionality is a massive first step to becoming a theologically savvy woman. Once you have your *approaches* right, the next thing is to simply begin reading. There are dozens of great Bible study methods out there for you to choose from, but one of our favorites is the simple GIPCP method. All you need is your Bible and a notebook. You begin by choosing any book of the Bible to read. As you read (starting from the beginning), take notes in your journal of the following five things:

GOD: How is the character of God and/or the gospel on display in this passage?

INSTRUCTION: What is being taught and communicated here?

PRAISE: What praises can I offer to God based on what I'm reading?

CONFESSION: In what ways am I disobeying God's Word or not worshiping Him as I should?

PRAYER: Based on today's study, how should my heart respond in prayer?

We hope this method is helpful for you. But just remember, "Whatever approach you take to reading the Bible," says Nancy DeMoss Wolgemuth, "don't let yourself become a slave to the method. Don't get so caught up in the mechanics that you miss the point. Remember that the goal is not how fast you can get through the Bible. The goal is to get the Word into your heart and life and to cultivate an intimate relationship with Jesus, the living Word of God."[3]

The greatest blessing in all of this, as we study the Bible, is that we would come to know and love the Author of this book ourselves. That our minds would be filled not just with knowledge of the Word but with worship of our Savior. He should be our greatest pursuit and deepest delight. The more you learn to treasure God's Word, the more you will treasure *Him*.

May we become a generation of women who join the psalmist in saying, "As a deer pants for flowing streams, so pants my soul for you, O God" (Ps. 42:1).

No More Dancing Mickeys

Our local churches and families would be greatly blessed and edified if we became a generation of biblically savvy women who know the Word of God for ourselves and who are serious about understanding and applying theology. Women who are done falling prey to crafty schemes and are ready to pursue God's Word with urgency and depth. Women who are eager to bring godly wisdom into our homes, relationships, and communities. Women who long to know our Savior deeply and intimately. Women who are tired of blindly falling into *ditches*.

Are you tired of accepting weak and wimpy womanhood as the norm and ready to become a wise and mature woman of the faith? Ephesians 4 is calling you to this aim: "that we may no longer be children, tossed to and fro by the waves and carried about by every wind of doctrine, by human cunning, by craftiness in deceitful schemes. Rather, speaking the truth in love, we are to grow up in every way into him who is the head, into Christ" (vv. 14–15).

It's time to call out the dancing Mickeys for what they are and become *theologically savvy women*.

Chapter 5 Study Guide

"Our local churches and families would be greatly blessed and edified if we became a generation of biblically savvy women who know the Word of God for ourselves and who are serious about understanding and applying theology."

1. Have you ever been tricked by a crafty scheme? If so, what happened?

_____

_____

2. When it comes to your current methods for studying the Bible, how would you rate the quality of your time in the Word?

   a. Deep, thorough, and intentional.

   b. Somewhat in depth.

   c. Bouncing around from passage to passage.

   d. Surface-level and shallow.

   e. I'm not really getting into the Word consistently right now.

   f. I don't know how to read my Bible.

3. When you hear the word _theology_, what comes to mind? Why?

   _____

   _____

4. Look back at the three *less helpful* and *helpful* approaches for studying the Bible. Which ones do you need to stop doing, and which do you need to start doing?

5. Why is it important for you to understand and know God's Word for yourself?

6. Name three things you can begin doing this week to move toward becoming a savvy woman of the Word:

   a.

   b.

   c.

chapter 6

Made to Be He and She

The road trip felt like it would never end. We'd been driving all day and were tired, "hangry" (hungry + angry), and ready to be home. With a few hours left, I (Kristen) asked if we could make one last bathroom stop. With Bethany, my mom, and a few other family members in the car, we took the next exit.

At this point, we were in the middle of nowhere-land, deep in the heart of west Texas. It was dark outside, and the only open gas station had a rundown building with sketchy lighting. My imagination ran wild as all those true crime podcasts I had listened to popped into my mind. But my bladder quickly shocked me back to reality and reminded me of my urgent need. I rushed inside, reassuring myself that there was only a slim chance of getting murdered. As I walked into the women's restroom, I grabbed the first stall available and quickly shut the door. The bathroom was quiet, and I assumed I was the only person in there. Relief washed over me. Then, out of nowhere, I heard someone with a low voice clear their throat a few stalls over.

I froze.

True crime stories came flooding back into my mind. *Who is in here with me? What if it's a mass murderer hiding out in the women's restroom waiting for some naive and unsuspecting woman like me to come in?*

With my heart pounding, I knew I needed to stay calm and rational. So I decided to pull the old "peekaboo, who are you?" maneuver by quietly looking under the stall wall. I needed to see the feet of that person. I had to know (1) if they were hiding in the stall by standing on the toilet seat waiting to kill me and (2) if this was in fact a woman and not a man.

So, quietly leaning down (without letting my hair touch the floor), I glanced a few stalls over, trying to get a glimpse of the mystery person's feet. What I saw caused a silent gasp to escape my lips.

That person was no woman.

The shoes were definitely men's shoes, and they were huge.

Feeling too terrified to even flush, I knew I had to get out of that bathroom ASAP. I would make a run for it. My stall was closest to the exit. After silently counting to three in my head, I burst out the door and ran into the main area of the gas station. My mom had just entered.

Rushing over to her, I told her about the creepy man in the bathroom and how I had barely escaped. Since this was the only gas station around for miles, we had no choice but to stay. My mom also desperately needed to use the bathroom. So she did what any strong, protective, and bold mother would do. She marched right over to the only man working behind the counter and told him there was a scary man hiding in the women's bathroom.

Surprised by this news, he got up and quickly walked straight over to the ladies' restroom. Opening the door halfway and leaning inside, he firmly called out, "Excuse me, sir?"

No answer.

"Umm, hello, sir?"

No answer again.

He tried a third time.

Still no response.

He walked over to us with a questioning look.

"There *is* a man in there!" I said emphatically.

He walked back over to the restroom, opened the door again, and loudly asked, "Excuse me . . . but is there a man in this bathroom?"

Silence filled the air for a few seconds; then, to our shock, a low but feminine voice loudly answered back: "I'm a woman."

Three simple words.

A woman? Now we were more intrigued than scared. We had to see who this person was.

After we lingered in the gas station a few more minutes, our mystery person was finally revealed.

It *was* a woman, indeed. A normal, everyday, average-height woman. And her shoes? After we saw her husband outside by their car, it became clear what was happening. He was a huge dude. He had large feet. Apparently, she was borrowing *his shoes* for her bathroom run inside.

Feeling relieved that our story wasn't going to become a future episode on a true crime podcast, we wrapped things up and got in the car. Bursting into laughter, we all felt deeply relieved that our "mass murderer" was, in fact, just an average, everyday woman.

And probably a nice one at that.

I'm a Woman

That three-word statement, *I'm a woman*, has stuck with us to this day. It's so simple and yet so profound. It carries with it so much significance, purpose, and meaning.

For centuries, this phrase has been clearly understood and confidently defined by civilizations. For the majority of human history, the phrase *I'm a woman* held the common and yet beautiful truth of someone who was born a *female*. It was universally attributed to those of the human population who were, in fact, made to be *she*. As technology advanced, we were even able to determine that girl babies are typically born with two X chromosomes, while boy babies typically have one X and one Y.

But in today's cultural climate, you don't have to look far to see that gender has been radically redefined. A person's gender is no longer considered fixed but is now "fluid." Modern medical doctors don't flinch at affirming a person's desire to become the other gender. Celebrities, political leaders, and media members have normalized terms like *nonbinary* and *gender nonconforming*, which seems to have ushered in a wave of experimentation among young people. Highly educated Ivy League professors insist that their students make known their preferred personal pronouns in class. Gone are the days when statements like *I'm a woman* could be taken at face value.

To our detriment, the line between what it means to be male and what it means to be female has been erased. The unique aspects of manhood and womanhood are being downplayed and outright ignored. We're told that there is no difference between men and women. That gender is simply a social construct invented by culture. Things like femininity and masculinity are nothing more than interchangeable gender expressions that any person can adopt.

This type of thinking is seeping into our churches and Christian homes too. With the foundation of feminist ideology and progressive Christianity in place, many churches are dismissing the biblical distinctions for male and female roles as nothing more than translation preferences. We've chosen to embrace what feels right rather than what *is right*. As a result, our Christian homes function more like non-Christian ones. Biblical distinctions for husbands, wives, fathers, and mothers aren't considered important or valuable anymore.

Gone are the days when statements like _I'm a woman_ could be taken at face value.

Rather than approaching God's Word with a desire to be informed by it, we approach God's Word with a heart to *inform it*.

But what we don't realize when we choose to rewrite the gender script on our own terms is that we're missing out on two crucial things:

1. A key piece to understanding who we are
2. A key piece to understanding who God is

Gender isn't a neutral concept randomly thrown together by our Creator but rather a complex design fashioned after the very image of God. The male and female genders carry within their design one of the keys to unlocking human identity and purpose. Gender carries within it magnificent and eternal truths that teach us about the very nature of our Creator.

This is why gender matters so much.

When we get gender wrong, we get *our identity* wrong and we get *God* wrong. Nothing makes sense anymore.

As you read these words right now, you are not a random person with a fluid gender identity. You are a woman. Handcrafted by God. Designed to be a female on purpose and for a purpose. You are made in the very image of God as a reflection of His nature. You are made to be *she* for God's glory and your good.

Woven within God's design for manhood and womanhood is a beautiful and eternally significant story. In fact, it's our origin story. And it all started one day, many centuries ago, when God created the first humans in a perfect garden called Eden. Picking up dirt from the newly formed ground, God began revealing His story for gender as He handcrafted the very first *man*.

Made to Be He

Imagine this scene: A lush garden filled with colorful trees and ripe fruit. Animals run to and fro, frolicking in the babbling brook. A gentle breeze softly blows through the tall grass. The sun is warm and life-giving. Everything is perfect in this place of paradise.

Welcome to the garden of Eden.

Well, at least the Eden we imagine in our minds. And we're probably not too far off. This place was stunning and perfect in every way. This would be the home of the soon-to-be newlyweds, Mr. and Mrs. Adam and Eve. But they're not here yet. In fact, this garden isn't even here yet. Because these humans don't exist. Everything in the world has been made, except for this magnificent garden and its new homeowners.

The Lord is ready, though. Reaching down with His own hands, He picks up fresh dirt from the ground. He then uses that rich, earthy soil to handcraft the first human being. Forming every part like a sculpture, fine-tuning His masterpiece, He makes the first human. God breathes into his nostrils the very breath of life (Gen. 2:7). If gender-reveal parties were a thing back then, blue confetti would have burst from the sky. Surprise! It's a boy! A *man*, in fact. A male human being. The very first of its kind.

Right here, in this spectacular moment, we glimpse the very first detail of God's plan and design for gender. He created a man. A fully developed guy with all the male attributes—strong muscles, testosterone, male reproductive organs, and a masculine frame. He was a man's man.

Taking a closer look at Genesis 2, we can see six attributes of manhood that God intentionally wove into His male creation.

Six Core Attributes of Manhood

1. Masculinity

As we just saw, Adam was created to be a *man*. He was a *he*. A male in every way. God could have created any sort of creature or being that He desired . . . but He intentionally chose to create a man. Adam's masculine build, strong frame, and testosterone-driven body were God-designed indicators of his role to come. Adam's manhood was handcrafted by God in the likeness of His very image (see Gen. 1:26–27).

2. Responsibility

Here's something we don't like to talk about much. The male was created *first* (see Gen. 2:5–9). That means he is the firstborn of all humankind. In biblical times, the first-born son held a huge responsibility in the Hebrew family. He carried the weight of his father's authority and was responsible for his siblings in a unique way. Woven into his birth position was the expectation of leadership, initiative, and the oversight of those in his care. Through Adam, God was setting the stage for His design for godly male leadership within the family (and one day, the church; see 1 Tim. 2:13; Titus 1:5–9).

This position doesn't make men more valuable than women; it simply points to God's intent for men to be godly leaders within their families and communities.

3. Godly Headship

Next, something interesting happens that most of us gloss over. When we look at Genesis 2, it appears that God creates Adam outside of the garden of Eden, *then* places him inside of it (see v. 8). Nothing God does is random or unintentional, so what's happening here? It seems that the Lord is bringing Adam into his home—his very own place—to be head of his new family unit. We see this pattern revealed later in this chapter, where we read, "A man shall leave his father and his mother and hold fast to his wife" (v. 24).

Adam leaves the place of his origin and moves into his new home to prepare for his family. We see this role of godly headship unpacked further in Ephesians 5.

4. Provision and Protection

After placing Adam in the garden, God commissions him to "work it and keep it" (Gen. 2:15). This new home isn't to be a place for the first dude to just sit idly by, chilling all day, eating tangerines. No way. La-Z-Boy recliners didn't even exist yet. God gives the man the role of maintaining the garden (work it) and protecting it (keep it). Long before the first woman is on the scene, God is teaching Adam the value of hard work, providing for his family, and protecting his homestead.

5. Spiritual Leadership

Adam seems to be a quick learner, but he's not ready yet. God needs to have a conversation with him first. Speaking directly to his face, God carefully explains the rules of the garden to Adam (see Gen. 2:16–17). This is a serious moment. God gives Adam the responsibility of receiving these important commands and explains the consequences for disobeying them. As head of his soon-to-be family, it's Adam's job to understand and share these important commands with his wife and lead her in following God. He is to be a godly spiritual leader for Eve by guiding her in the truths and commands of the Lord (we see godly spiritual leadership reiterated in Eph. 5:25–26).

6. Godly Authority and Initiative

With the ground rules laid, God has one more thing to teach Adam—how to exercise godly authority. In Genesis

2:19–20, God brings all the animals to Adam and gives him the unique responsibility of naming each kind. Can you imagine this scene? Thousands of animals lining up for Adam, waiting to receive their name. "Umm . . . you shall be called . . . kangaroo!" *Perfect.* "And you . . . how about . . . umm . . . hippo!" *Yes. Nailed it.*

God is mentoring Adam in what it means to exercise godly authority. He's giving him the opportunity to lead and care for the things he has been entrusted with (again, Titus 2 affirms this call to godly authority).

As the last penguin waddles away, Adam notices something striking. Every animal has an opposite of its own kind . . . but he has nobody. We don't know how Adam felt at this moment, but there was probably a sense of deep longing and yearning inside of him.

For the first time, God says that something *isn't good*. "Then the LORD God said, 'It is not good that the man should be alone; I will make him a helper fit for him'" (Gen. 2:18). God surveyed all He had made and knew Adam's preparation and training were complete. Adam was ready to receive his precious bride.

Putting the man into a deep sleep, God drew out a rib from Adam's side as the building block for His new creation (vv. 21–22). The first woman would come from the very bones and flesh of her man.

The first *he* was about to meet the very first *she*.

Made to Be She

Imagine what it might have looked like for Adam to meet Eve for the first time.

With his eyes slowly blinking open, Adam feels a gentle breeze caress his face. The trees sway above him. The sun peeks through the clouds, warming his skin. Raking his hand through his hair, he slowly stands to his feet. Hearing the sound of soft footsteps behind him, he turns around to see God walking toward him in the garden.

But . . . *wait*.

God isn't walking alone. There's something—no, *someone*—with Him.

Squinting to get a better look, Adam is amazed by what he sees. *Could it be?* Coming close, God brings this exquisitely gorgeous creature right up to Adam. You can almost feel the sheer joy in his voice as he realizes *who* this new being is. *Whoa, baby.*

He bursts out, "This at last is bone of my bones and flesh of my flesh; she shall be called Woman, because she was taken out of Man" (v. 23). He immediately recognizes the significance of this creature. Eve is not a *he* but a *she*. A beautiful and breathtaking female.

Genesis reveals six distinct attributes of womanhood.

Six Core Attributes of Womanhood

1. Femininity

Eve is a *female*. A *she*. Everything about her is different from Adam. She is his counterpart. His complement. His magnificent opposite. She has firm but feminine muscles, breathtaking curves, and the unique ability to bear children. She was created equal in worth and value but different in makeup and function. She is not a man but a woman—full of estrogen, fertility, and femininity.

2. Ability to Produce Life

Unlike Adam, Eve was given the unique gift and ability to bring new life into the world. This wasn't an afterthought by God but an intentional part of His design and function for the female. From the beginning, Eve was created with a womb, fallopian tubes, eggs, and monthly cycles. Her reproductive abilities stood in complete contrast to Adam's. By God's intentional design, pregnancy would occur only as the male moved his body toward the female's body. As the female receives his pursuit, the possibility for new life occurs. This is incredible. Even within the sexual design, we see the male and female distinctions being played out as the man *pursues* and the woman *responds*.

Eve did not view her reproductive design as a burdensome physical reality to overcome. She did not compare her body to Adam's. She joyfully received God's good plan for her femininity and viewed her reproduction as a blessing.

3. Softness

When you dig a little deeper into the original language behind Adam's declaration in Genesis 2:23 ("She shall be called Woman, because she was taken out of Man"), you'll discover something amazing. The Hebrew words for man and woman in this verse are *ish* and *ishsha*. They come from the root meaning "strength" and "soft."[1] Essentially, Adam is declaring that the man represents strength and the woman represents softness. They are complementary opposites. He is the strong protector, fighting on behalf of his family. She is his feminine opposite, with the unique capacity to nurture and bring forth life.

If you've ever wondered why chick flicks and fairy-tale stories resonate so much with women, it's right here in Genesis. Woven within the very DNA of the female design is a softness that responds favorably to a man's strength and protection.

4. Responsiveness toward Godly Leadership

As Adam gently takes the hand of his bride, you can imagine the love, beauty, and romance as he says something like, "I'm so glad you're mine. Come on! I'll show you everything you need to know about the garden."

Eve loves him. She knows she was created for him. She knows Adam is the firstborn and the head of their family. She doesn't push against his position but embraces it joyfully.

Even when Adam takes the initiative right off the bat of naming her ("she shall be called woman"), Eve embraces this. She doesn't protest by saying, "Hold on, Mr. Dude—I'll name myself, thank you very much!" No. She willingly embraces her new husband's loving care for her and welcomes his leadership. Eve thrives in her relationship with Adam.

5. Relational Connection

The fact that she was made *for* the man also reveals something else. She was created with a highly relational bent. Connecting through relationships is a core part of her design.

Think about the difference here. Adam was created first, outside of the garden, then brought into the garden and given the job of working the ground and protecting his home. Eve was made second, inside the garden, then given to the man within the safety of their home to be in a relationship with him. Working, providing for, and protecting the family were placed on the man in a unique way that they were not on the woman.

Now, that doesn't mean that work isn't important or valuable to the woman. It just reveals that "her identity isn't based on work nearly as much as on how well she connects in her relationships."[2] She is the one given the ability to bear new life and nurture those relationships in a unique way. Our culture pushes the message that dads and moms are the same. That the male and female are interchangeable. But right here in Genesis, we see a different story.

6. Helping the Man Glorify God

Now, this next point about womanhood is one that usually gets most women's feathers ruffled. It's in Genesis 2:18, where the Lord says, "It is not good that the man should be alone; I will make him a helper fit for him."

Did you catch that last part? The h-word? Yes. It's there. *Helper*. But before you close this book or throw it across the room, hear us out. The word *helper* once ruffled our feathers too because we didn't understand its true meaning or purpose. Feminist ideology has instilled in our minds a gag reflex to anything that remotely sounds like female inferiority. But that's where they get this wrong.

God did not create Eve as an inferior being to help Adam. She wasn't created to be his servant, fetching his slippers while he chills in his recliner. In this passage, the word *helper* is not a demeaning term at all. In fact, the Hebrew word for helper (*ezer*) is a powerful one. In the Bible, it's most often used to describe the Lord being our *helper* (Ps. 33:20; 72:12). If the Lord is referenced as our helper, then we know it is not a term given to a "lesser being."

As Mary Kassian explains, "in order for us to understand the implications of the woman's 'helper' design, we need to consider what the woman is to 'help' the man do. The male was created to bring glory to God—and to serve Him (rather than himself). God created a helper to assist the man in fulfilling his ultimate purpose. Woman helps man glorify God in a way he could not do if she did not exist."[3]

Manhood and womanhood—*together*—help put the glory of God on display.

Say Hello to Estrogen and Testosterone

Raising two boys has given me (Kristen) a whole new perspective on the male species. It has become even more clear to me that men and women are not wired the same way. When our oldest son turned thirteen, my husband decided to take him on a special trip to celebrate his growth into manhood. Grabbing their backpacks, tent, and hunting bows, they headed for a remote national forest in northern Colorado.

They spent a week wearing camouflage clothes and hiking around an uninhabited land with access to nothing more than the packs on their backs and nature's streams for water. They didn't shower, change their underwear, or have access to anything modern the entire time.

And they absolutely loved it.

The sheer excitement of the elk hunt drove them forward day after day. Even though they didn't end up bringing home the meat, they loved the adventure and challenge of it all. There was something deep inside of them that fueled their desire to hunt, pursue, and conquer.

Despite the cultural narrative that pushes for gender sameness, we don't have to look far to see that men and women are not the same. Sure, we might enjoy some of the same hobbies, interests, and sports, but at our core, we are not often driven by the same things in the same ways. We're not saying that hunting is exclusively a man's sport—some women enjoy hunting as well. But, on average, men seem to gravitate toward this sport far more than women do. In fact, if you look at the statistics for the male-to-female ratio for hunting, the numbers tell an interesting story. Currently, 94.3 percent of hunting guides in the US are *males*, while only 5.7 percent are females.[4]

This isn't a random accident. It speaks to our differing drives and inclinations.

If you're married, you see these differences every day in your relationship. If you have a son, a brother, a dad, or guy friends, you see it there too. We are not wired exactly the same.

In these modern days, medical science and technology have only revealed how truly different we are.

By God's design, the male body stands in contrast to the female body. Everything, from our differing shapes, muscle mass, and hormone levels to our sexual reproductive organs, points to our complementary designs as man and woman. Our secular world dismisses these differences as unimportant details. But our bodies reveal huge truths about who we are and our roles as male and female. Our physical designs affirm the six core attributes of manhood and womanhood we just saw in Genesis.

Mary Kassian tells us in *True Woman 101* that, on average,

> men have 50 percent greater total muscle mass, based on weight, than do women. A woman who is the same size as her male counterpart is generally only 80 percent as strong. A woman's body is much more efficient at storing energy (fat) to give her reserves for pregnancy and lactation. Men have large hearts and lungs and greater amounts of red blood cells. When a man is jogging at about 50 percent of his capacity, a woman will need to work over 70 percent of her capacity to keep up. The female body produces a large quantity of a hormone called oxytocin, which promotes bonding and affiliation and enhances maternal instinct. The male body produces large quantities of testosterone, which create the push to advance, take risks, guard, and conquer.[5]

The man's physical body and hormonal drive help him accomplish his job of providing for and protecting his family. With twenty times more testosterone surging through his veins than a female, he was created to conquer, fight, and pursue.[6]

In contrast, a woman's body runs on estrogen. This hormone gives women a deeper desire for emotional connection. It has even been called the *connecting* hormone.

During a woman's fertile years, the female body has fluctuating hormone levels that change four times every month during her cycle.[7] If you've ever wondered why your emotions feel like a roller coaster, that may be why. The changing hormone levels might not feel like a gift, but they are a monthly reminder that a woman's uterus exists and that she has the unique ability to bring new life into the world.

In her book *Let Me Be a Woman*, Elisabeth Elliot writes, "Yours is the body of a woman. What does it signify? Is there invisible meaning in its visible signs—the softness, the smoothness, the lighter bone and muscle structure, the breasts, the womb? Are they utterly unrelated to what you yourself are? Isn't your identity intimately bound up with these material forms?"[8]

Our female body points to our identity and purpose.

These core characteristics of womanhood do not mean that every woman will get married or that every married woman will birth babies. Marriage and children are blessings, but they do not define a woman's worth or ability to glorify God in her femininity. We are all daughters of God first, and our call to glorify Him remains our foundational purpose in every season of life.

> Marriage and children are blessings, but they do not define a woman's worth or ability to *glorify* God in her femininity.

The more the two of us have learned about the physical and hormonal differences between men and women, the more blown away we are by God's design. From the beginning of time, He knew exactly what He was doing when He created them *male and female*.

Stepping into God-Defined Womanhood

Do you remember when those one-size-fits-all shirts were really popular? I (Bethany) was out shopping during this era and came across a rack full of these. Holding up one of the tiny, scrunched-up shirts, I assumed it was doll clothing. It looked miniature. But then I saw the sign. "One size fits all." *There is no way*, I thought to myself. Testing this theory, I picked up a shirt and began stretching it out. To my shock, the tiny, scrunched-up shirt kept getting bigger. And bigger. And bigger! When I had it fully stretched out, I stood there corrected. *One size really does fit all.*

As we've been exploring God's design for gender through the lens of Genesis, we can see that His plan for femininity is similar. Regardless of your age, your season of life, where you live in the world, your personality type, or your background, the six attributes of womanhood are something you can put on with God's strength and grace. Here's a recap of what we saw in Genesis.

Femininity is at the core of God's design for womanhood.
Producing life is at the core of God's design for womanhood.
Softness is at the core of God's design for womanhood.

> **Responsiveness toward godly leadership** is at the core of God's design for womanhood.
>
> **Relational connection** is at the core of God's design for womanhood.
>
> **Helping the man glorify God** is at the core of God's design for womanhood.

God's design was made to fit each one of us. It's universally applicable. It's not a cookie-cutter mold, forcing us to look exactly the same externally, but rather a way of living and thinking that is shaped by God's truth. Even if a woman never gets married or has kids, she can still nurture relationships, produce spiritual life, and glorify God in her femininity. As Christian women, our lives will look vastly different across the globe, but there should be a recognizable godly, feminine disposition that is beautifully visible within each one of us.

Instead of doing things our own way, God is calling us (His daughters) to trust Him. To reject the lie that we know better than He does. To put off the false paths of feminist womanhood and religious womanhood, and instead walk in the truth of what He has revealed through His Word.

Yes, sin has marred our womanhood. The relationship between the man and the woman has been broken by the fall. But thanks be to Jesus, we are being redeemed. By God's grace, our lives should reflect the redeemed version of womanhood we have in Christ. One that has been covered by the blood of Jesus and is being sanctified to reflect our Maker.

One that is strong not because of our own strength but because of how tightly we're clinging to our Savior.

As Mary Kassian so eloquently puts it, "God created gender, manhood and womanhood, to image who he is. Gender displays God. That's what gender does. Who we are and how we relate as women and men is an object lesson. It's a parable. It tells a very important story, and the story isn't about us. Scripture says that God created sons and daughters for his glory, to display the jaw-dropping wonder of who he is."[9]

Womanhood isn't ultimately about us but about us following our Savior and pointing others back to the incredible God who made us.

Chapter 6 Study Guide

"Manhood and womanhood—*together*—help put the glory of God on display."

1. If you had to describe what it means to be a *woman*, what would you say?

   _____

   _____

2. After taking a deep dive into God's design for the male and female in Genesis 2, what stood out to you the most?

   _____

   _____

3. Out of the six attributes of manhood, which one do you find most interesting, and why?

   _____

   _____

4. Out of the six attributes of womanhood, which one do you find most interesting, and why?

   _____

   _____

5. Which attribute of womanhood do you find most challenging to embrace? Circle your answer.

   a. **Femininity** is at the core of God's design for womanhood.

   b. **Producing life** is at the core of God's design for womanhood.

   c. **Softness** is at the core of God's design for womanhood.

   d. **Responsiveness toward godly leadership** is at the core of God's design for womanhood.

   e. **Relational connection** is at the core of God's design for womanhood.

   f. **Helping the man glorify God** is at the core of God's design for womanhood.

   Why do you find that specific attribute challenging to embrace?

   _____

   _____

6. Take a moment to write your own prayer of surrender to God, asking Him to help you embrace His good design for your womanhood.

   _____

   _____

chapter 7

God's Radical Design for Marriage and Sex

I t's a girl!" This was the fifth time our parents heard those words. First with Kristen, second with Bethany, third with Ellissa, fourth with Rebekah, and now fifth with Suzanna. Five daughters and a ton of estrogen. We were officially a modern-day retelling of the classic *Pride and Prejudice*.

Imagine being our father and realizing you have to marry off not one, not two, not three, not four, but five daughters. Five times giving your blessing. Five times walking down the aisle. Five times hearing the pastor's question, "Who gives this woman to be with this man?" and responding, "Her mother and I." Five times watching your baby girl walk in with your name and leave with his.

Not to mention, we also have three brothers. That's right. Eight siblings in all. We would say our poor parents had their hands full, but I'm pretty sure they knew what they were getting themselves into. They loved having a big family.

The first wedding among us sisters was mine (Kristen's). It was 2011, and I was finally getting my happily ever after. Everything about this wedding carried the combined hopes and dreams of us five sisters. We went all out for this wedding. Every detail was perfectly planned. Nothing went untouched. From the centerpieces at the reception to the decorations in the honeymoon suite, we didn't miss a thing. We Baird sisters (our maiden name) loved romance, and we loved an elaborate wedding.

While Kristen traveled on her honeymoon, I (Bethany) dreamed of the day when my own Prince Charming would sweep me off my feet. Surely the rest of us sisters would follow shortly in Kristen's footsteps and steadily get married over the next decade. Right? Wrong. Year after year after year passed by, and none of us were even close to tying the knot. I couldn't understand why God would withhold such a good gift from me. I valued marriage. I rejoiced when other couples got married. So, why was God holding out on me?

This "romance drought" (as we sisters liked to call it) forced us to do some soul-searching and really question our understanding of dating, marriage, and sex. Why did we want to get married? What was the purpose of it? Why is sex reserved for marriage? With no weddings to plan and plenty of time on our hands, we started doing our research on the meaning of romantic relationships. First with books on dating, then books on marriage, and ultimately digging into the theology of what marriage truly represents.

This time of study was eye-opening. I had no idea how shallow my view was. Yes, I had been doing the whole "wait until marriage" thing, but I didn't truly understand the depths of what marriage and sex actually represented. I didn't understand how my being a woman and marrying a man represented the gospel. I didn't understand how the very makeup of the male and female sexual anatomy points to a greater gospel reality. Yeah, let that one sink in for a minute.

> I didn't understand how the very makeup of the male and female sexual anatomy points to a greater *gospel* reality.

My romance drought officially ended on October 14, 2018, when I walked down the aisle to my handsome groom and entered into a lifelong covenant with my husband. The love bug caught fire, because our family went from seven years of drought to having four weddings (three daughters and one son) in the course of four years.

The best part of these new marriages wasn't the venue, the great food, the guests, or the bride's dress. The best part was how intentional each couple was to build their relationship on a biblical understanding of love. Especially as it's getting harder and harder to build a relationship on such a solid foundation.

Are You My Soulmate?

He's single. She's lonely. Fate has brought them together. The rest of the movie is filled with steamy love scenes and glamorized visions of romance. It doesn't matter that they've built their entire relationship on infatuation and emotion. The viewer watching this blockbuster romance is made to believe that a strong sexual connection is the key to true and lasting love.

This same story has been portrayed over and over again. From the classic animated movies to the bestselling novels. True love is all about finding your soulmate and being with the one who makes you feel a certain way. If you're happy, it's love. If you're no longer happy, you've fallen out of love. If you're married but attracted to someone else, you're not with your soulmate. If you're a woman and prefer to be with a woman, you must satisfy that longing. Hollywood has created a self-centered, temporal, and truly meaningless version of love. They've created their own picture of marriage and have blasted it across movie screens to be absorbed by happiness-seeking viewers.

Do any of these statements sound familiar to you?

Just follow your heart and it will lead you to your soulmate.

True love is all about feeling in love.

If you have to work at the relationship, it's not meant to be.

True love should come easy.

He should make you happy all the time.

When the spark fades, you need to move on.

Commitment is conditional.

If you're no longer happy, you need to move on.

That is the essence of Hollywood's version of love. It looks good on the silver screen, but it's a mess when lived out in real life. And it's not just the secular world that's being affected. It's marriages within the church too. I (Kristen) remember a Christian friend of mine sharing with me how glad she was that one of her best friends was getting divorced. "They're just not the same people they were when they first got married. It's time for them to move on." This is a woman who's bought into the idea that personal happiness is the foundation of a relationship. Everything hinges on whether or not happiness is present. Am I happy? Do they make me feel good? If the answer is yes, then I stay. If the answer is no, it's time to move on.

Many Christian couples are building their relationships on this shallow understanding of marriage and hoping they will have a love that lasts. They're redefining marriage according to their own happiness terms. Many Christians have taken it even further than this, though. A man with a man. A woman with a woman. A believer with a nonbeliever. It's totally up to self to decide what marriage means and what love is.

> *Sex. Pleasure. Redemption. Covenant. Sacrifice. Mystery.* These are words that describe the *beauty* of a God-defined marriage.

If this is what God had in mind, He could have just added it to Scripture. "Love is love. Happiness is love. Love is a feeling." But He didn't. When God created the institution of marriage, He had something much more cosmic and romantic in mind.

Sex. Pleasure. Redemption. Covenant. Sacrifice. Mystery. These are words that describe the beauty of a God-defined marriage. It's so much more than happiness. It's so much more than a feeling. It's so much more than temporal pleasure. God's design for marriage is beyond imagination and ultimately reflects the greatest love story ever told.

I Need a Better View

A few years ago, I (Bethany) was at a bachelorette party for a good friend of mine. She planned a classy weekend, with brunch, canvas painting, and a good old, classic romance movie. Although I love my friend, I do not love canvas painting. Art and I just don't go well together. I sweat bullets during a game of Pictionary just hoping someone will be able to identify my drawing of an ant or a ladybug. So you can imagine the sweat I was dripping when we signed up to paint an intricate field of flowers.

The seats were preassigned at the studio, and the instructor welcomed us as we filed in. Somehow I got stuck in the one seat that had a pillar blocking the view to the front of the room. I was struggling to keep my eye on the original painting as I attempted to re-create it. To make matters worse, the instructor continued to come my way and give me pointers. I wanted to shout, *I know! My painting looks like a toddler's work of art. Please leave me alone. This isn't my specialty.* I just smiled and nodded until he walked away. Let's just say my painting didn't quite make it as a piece of art in my home. I tossed that bad boy in the garbage where it belonged.

Building a marriage is similar to sitting in a canvas-painting class. There is an original piece of art for marriage, and it's described to us in detail in Scripture. We're tasked with focusing on the original and doing our best to reflect what the designer has displayed for us. Just like with canvas painting, the goal is to mimic the original to create the best work of art possible. In order to reflect the original, we have to know exactly what it looks like.

We took a deep dive into the creation story and the making of man and woman in the previous chapter. Let's fast-forward to the New Testament and take a look at what this marriage relationship is all about. There is no better place to turn than Ephesians 5. Paul wrote this letter to the church in Ephesus as a general instruction on what marriage was supposed to look like and the gospel picture it reflected. This church needed clear instruction on how to live set apart in a pagan society that had rejected a biblical view of marriage.

Thousands of years later, we're in need of the exact same teachings as the people from Ephesus.

> Wives, submit to your own husbands, as to the Lord. For the husband is the head of the wife even as Christ is the head of the church, his body, and is himself its Savior. Now as the church submits to Christ, so also wives should submit in everything to their husbands.
>
> Husbands, love your wives, as Christ loved the church and gave himself up for her, that he might sanctify her, having cleansed her by the washing of water with the word, so that he might present the church to himself in splendor, without spot or wrinkle or any such thing, that she might be holy and without blemish. In the same way husbands should love their wives as their own bodies. He who loves his wife loves himself. For no one ever hated his own flesh, but nourishes and cherishes it, just as Christ does the church, because we are members of his body. "Therefore a man shall leave his father and mother and hold fast to his wife, and the two shall become one flesh." This mystery is profound, and I am saying that it refers to Christ and the church. (5:22–32)

Whoa. The wife in this passage is getting some amazing love. Who wouldn't want a man like that? Sign us up. Throughout this passage, one thing is very clear. There is one man and one woman. One groom and one bride. There is a male and there is a female. And that's not accidental. Everything about God's design for marriage has purpose and meaning. The husband (the man/the groom) is given instruction on exactly what his role is in a marriage. The wife (the woman/the bride) is given a beautiful vision of how she represents the church. Both roles represent something beyond themselves. Let's break it down.

He Is the Head of His Wife. She Submits as the Church Does to Christ.

Verses 22–24: Wives, submit to your own husbands, as to the Lord. For the husband is the head of the wife even as Christ is the head of the church, his body, and is himself its Savior. Now as the church submits to Christ, so also wives should submit in everything to their husbands.

God is a God of order. Down to the very details of roles within marriage. We are not left to wonder about His plan and order for a husband and wife. It's crucial to understand that *submission* is not a "lesser-than" word. I love how the pastors and theologians at GotQuestions.org unpack this biblical reality. They say, "*Submit* is not a bad word. Submission is not a reflection of inferiority or lesser worth. Christ constantly submitted Himself to the will of the Father (Luke 22:42; John 5:30), without giving up an iota of His worth." They go on to say, "A wife should submit to her husband, not because women are inferior (the Bible never teaches that), but because that is how God designed the marital relationship to function."[1]

It's crucial to note that the husband does not have free rein here. He is reflecting Christ, and we know that Christ constantly submitted Himself to the will of the Father. The wife isn't called to submit to every man but specifically to her husband. She reflects the church in the way the church submits to Christ. It's the start of the gospel image marriage displays.

He Reflects Christ. She Reflects the Church.

Verse 25: Husbands, love your wives, as Christ loved the church and gave himself up for her.

Who doesn't love a man being strong and sacrificing for his woman? There is a reason we love it. It's hardwired into our makeup. This is a husband's highest calling: to reflect Christ and love his bride in the same way that Christ loves the church. God uses the male/groom as a direct reflection of Christ and the female/bride as a direct reflection of His church (i.e., those who trust in Him as their Savior are the church). A groom's role represents Christ. It represents sacrifice. It represents giving up oneself. A bride's role represents response. It represents receiving. It represents being taken care of at the deepest level possible.

He Cares for Her Soul. She Receives His Discipleship.

Verse 26: . . . that he might sanctify her, having cleansed her by the washing of water with the word.

A husband's primary job is caring for the soul of his wife. He is called to nurture his wife by taking her to the Word and showing her the love of Christ. It's his job to come alongside her, open the Bible, and spend time nurturing her heart with the truth of Scripture. Umm . . . wow. Can you even imagine? Most husbands are unaware that this is a part of their literal job description. They are reflectors of Christ sanctifying the church. It's her job as the bride to receive this discipleship. To learn from her groom as he takes her to the Word and helps her to become sanctified. Just as Christ sanctifies the church, a husband helps sanctify his wife in the Word. There is deep and powerful meaning in their roles within marriage.

He Presents Her to Christ. She Is a Picture of Splendor.

Verse 27: . . . so that he might present the church to himself in splendor, without spot or wrinkle or any such thing, that she might be holy and without blemish.

Christ will one day present us (the church) in perfect purity and holiness to our heavenly Groom. A husband's job is to do the same with his wife. Preparing her heart and soul for the day she will stand before her Maker. Think of a wedding. The bride walks down in pure white and is the focus of the ceremony. She spends hours preparing herself to be presented to her groom. The doors open and we see a glowing bride and groom full of anticipation, waiting to enter that lifelong covenant. This wedding is only a picture of the greater wedding you're being prepared for. Your husband has the responsibility of preparing you for your eternal Groom and the wedding feast in heaven.

He Loves Completely. She Is Nourished and Cherished.

Verses 28–30: In the same way husbands should love their wives as their own bodies. He who loves his wife loves himself. For no one ever hated his own flesh, but nourishes and cherishes it, just as Christ does the church, because we are members of his body.

There is a direct connection between Christ giving of Himself for the church and a husband giving of himself for his wife. When a husband nourishes and cherishes the heart of his woman, he is reflecting the original image that God intended. He is mirroring the gospel. It's absurd that some people think the wife is subservient or "less than" in a Christian marriage. Everything about these verses mimics a husband sacrificing like Christ did for us. There is overwhelming sacrificial love in what Jesus did for us on the cross. In a similar way, this is what a Christian husband is called to. A wife is simply called to receive that sacrificial love.

He Pursues. She Responds. They Become One Flesh.

Verses 31–32: "Therefore a man shall leave his father and mother and hold fast to his wife, and the two shall become one flesh." This mystery is profound, and I am saying that it refers to Christ and the church.

The husband and wife leave their families of origin and become a new family unit, with a new purpose, together. The two of us love how pastor P.J. Tibayan describes their purpose: "She submits; he sacrifices. She follows; he leads. She affirms; he initiates. She reflects Jesus; he reflects Jesus. The greatest privilege in marriage is reflecting our Savior. And, in God's design, the privilege is equally great even though Jesus is reflected differently and uniquely by a husband and his wife."[2] Married couples are designed to experience the deepest form of sexual intimacy. The man's physical body reflects his greater calling. His body is designed to give, pursue, and ultimately sacrifice itself for his wife. Her body reflects her greater purpose as a wife and mirror of the church. She is physically designed to be pursued, to receive, and ultimately to create new life. Just like the church.

Sex Is a Celebration

Sex is a celebration of the marriage covenant. Did you know that? One of our married friends joked that she and her husband were going to have sex multiple times a day in their marriage to celebrate the covenant. Now, this is a woman who gets the bigger picture.

It only takes 0.46 seconds to get over 2,400,000,000 internet search results to the question "Is sex the best thing on earth?" The majority of articles and comments argue for the fact that a mutually satisfying sexual encounter is one of the best physical and emotional experiences on earth. Humans desire sex, but they often go about it in very broken and damaging ways. Most of us would agree that things like porn, erotica, and one-night stands are shallow substitutes for real marital intimacy. We can't experience the real thing, though, if we don't even know what the real thing is. Without a picture of something greater, we can't aim for that truly satisfying and authentic experience.

It wasn't until I (Bethany) was on that journey of discovering the true meaning of marriage that I also discovered God's design for sex. In fact, the two of us take a deep dive into all things intimacy inside our book *Sex, Purity, and the Longings of a Girl's Heart: Discovering the Beauty and Freedom of God-Defined Sexuality*. A must-read for all women. It will blow up your view of sex in the best way possible.

Honestly, it blew my mind when I realized the depths of why God created sex. One of my favorite Christian sex experts, Dr. Juli Slattery, explains it perfectly:

> God created sex for a lot of reasons—for procreation, for pleasure, for intimate knowing between a husband and wife. However, one of the most important reasons He created sex is to communicate about Himself. . . . God created sex and the covenant of marriage to be a brilliant metaphor of how deeply He knows us and longs for us to know Him. . . . Sexual intimacy is a powerful picture of the gospel—of the degree of intimacy and ecstasy we are capable of having with God. The Christian marriage is designed to be a showcase of this masterpiece. The romantic longings of a single woman mirror the longings of a bride who is waiting for the ultimate salvation—the coming of Jesus Christ. To the extent that our understanding and experience of sex is damaged and twisted, our view of God is compromised. Here's the takeaway: What you think about sex really matters. Having God's perspective on the topic, whether you are single or married, is a vital piece of your growth as a daughter of God.[3]

Understanding marriage and sex within the context of the gospel changes everything. It unlocks the greater reason for how a marriage relationship should be pursued. Sex is no longer just about physical passion. It's about understanding that we were made to be in a deep, all-knowing relationship with God. That is the true meaning of sex. That is the greater reason for your existence. To be in an intimate relationship with your Savior. This brings hope to every woman, whether single or married. Your greatest purpose isn't to have mind-blowing sex. Your greatest purpose is to be in an intimate relationship with your heavenly Groom.

The Gospel Is a Love Story

From Genesis to Revelation, the gospel story of marriage is painted for us. God in His creativity chose to use the male and the female to tell this story. He uses marriage between a man and a woman to tell His redemption plan. The gospel is a love story that starts with creation and ends with a wedding feast in heaven. Here's a picture of that love story from creation to the end of time.

> God creates a man and a woman and unites them in covenant marriage. The couple lives in perfect harmony with one another and with God. They experience deep, all-satisfying intimacy in every way possible. Everything is perfect (Gen. 2).
>
> The couple rebels against God, and intimacy is broken. Sin, shame, and guilt now plague the couple, and they no longer walk in the garden with God (Gen. 3).

After years of sin and broken relationship with God, the Groom (Jesus) is prophesied to come and save His people. This brings home that perfect intimacy can one day be restored (Isa. 7; 42; 61; Hosea 11; Mic. 5).

Jesus (the Groom) gives His life on the cross in pursuit of His people. Those who receive His invitation of new life in Him become His bride (the church) (John 1:12; 3:16–17; 1 Pet. 3:18).

Christ is in heaven, preparing a beautiful wedding feast for His bride (the church). One day all will be made perfect in this relationship when true intimacy is found in heaven at this wedding celebration (Ps. 16:11; John 14:2; Rev. 19:6–9).

The bride (His church) receives Jesus's sacrificial love and begins preparing for the day when she will be with her Groom (Jesus) again (Eph. 1:13; Rev. 19:7–9).

This is the gospel love story that marriage reflects. It's romantic. It's breathtaking. Christ pursued each one of us while we were still sinners. He loved us. He came after our hearts. He died for us. And He is preparing the ultimate wedding feast so that one day we can be united in perfect intimacy.

Your female identity in a marriage is so crucial. You are the reflection of the bride. There is no bride without a female. There is no groom without a male. God chose to use gender as the core part of His gospel love story. The very core of your biology is designed to reflect something greater than yourself. Whether you get married or remain single, you can celebrate God's goodness in His making you a female. You can champion the beauty of marriage even if you never get married. You can celebrate that you are daily being pursued by your Groom (Christ). Even if you never become a bride during your life on this earth, you have a Groom who is preparing a wedding feast for you in heaven.

Chapter 7 Study Guide

"From Genesis to Revelation, the gospel story of marriage is painted for us. God in His creativity chose to use the male and the female to tell this story."

1. Circle the statements that you have been told or have heard:

    Just follow your heart and it will lead you to your soulmate.

    True love is all about feeling in love.

    If you have to work at the relationship, it's not meant to be.

    True love should come easy.

    He should make you happy all the time.

    When the spark fades, you need to move on.

    Commitment is conditional.

    If you're no longer happy, you need to move on.

2. When God created the institution of marriage, He had something much more cosmic and romantic in mind. Write down the six words we used to describe this kind of marriage:

    a. _____

    b. _____

    c. _____

    d. _____

    e. _____

    f. _____

3. Who do the husband and the wife represent, according to Ephesians 5?

_____

_____

4. Sex is a _____ of the marriage covenant.

5. How does understanding marriage and sex within the context of the gospel change your perspective of relationships?

_____

_____

6. Describe how the gospel is a love story.

_____

_____

Part 3
THE SHAPING OF MODERN WOMANHOOD

chapter 8

When *She* Decides to Become *He*

We knew there would be protesters at the event. Exactly how many, we didn't know. It was 2015, and the landscape surrounding transgenderism was hot. The two of us decided to travel to a Christian training conference in Kentucky to become better equipped on the topic of sexuality. With Girl Defined Ministries having been founded less than a year before this, we were desperate for biblical guidance on how to discuss these intense issues with our community.

The protesters made it known well in advance that they were not fans of this conference and would be at the event with signs and banners to make their voices heard. They kept their promise. Protesters lined the streets as the conference attendees hurried into the building. Emotions were high, and none of us wanted things to escalate.

I (Bethany) made it safely inside and hurried to grab a seat. That's when I noticed a person at the end of my row. I tried to steal a glance without being rude. This person had broad shoulders and looked tall, even sitting down. They came dressed to impress with their neon high heels, hot-pink dress, and over-the-top makeup. It almost seemed like they were trying to attract looks in their direction.

When the first session ended, this person made a beeline for the speaker. The person wanted to talk and, it seemed, wanted everyone to see. They stood proudly in the middle of the aisle and in a deep, booming voice introduced themselves to the speaker.

Yep. It was a man. No doubt about it.

A man dressed in women's clothing. A man with fake breasts. A man with a wig. A man pretending to be a woman. Only . . . I don't think he was pretending. I think he really believed he was a she. Not a born she. A he who had altered his body, changed his clothing, and presented as a she.

He seemed to make it his personal mission to protest this conference from the inside out. He had purchased a ticket and was present at every single session. He continued to pursue the speakers and protest their viewpoints after each session. He continued to stand front and center before and after every session, ensuring that everyone saw him.

I'm not sure if he felt he accomplished his outcome or not. I don't know what the speakers said to him, and I don't know what they thought about his bold presence in the room. I just know that I was grateful for the conference and the encouragement it gave us to be bold in holding to God's truths on gender.

It's no secret that over the past decade the topic of transgenderism has become one of the hottest issues of our day.

Men and women have skyrocketed to fame simply by sharing their stories of transition on social media. Doctors and big pharma companies have raked in millions upon millions of dollars by performing these surgeries and offering medical assistance to the transgender community.[1]

Here's what's surprising, though: According to UCLA's Williams Institute, only about 1.4 percent of Americans identify as being transgender.[2] Despite the fact that those are insanely small numbers, the topic of transgenderism (and all that it entails) is easily one of the most popular, controversial, and dividing issues of our day.

Embracing transgenderism spits in the face of what God intended.

The reason this topic matters so much to the two of us (and should matter to you) is because transgenderism has become a war on God's good design for womanhood. Not just worldly womanhood but the womanhood that God created from the beginning. Embracing transgenderism spits in the face of what God intended.

Well-known journalist and author Abigail Shrier wrote an entire book outlining just how devastating transgenderism has become for girls and women. In her book *Irreversible Damage*, Shrier says,

> Between 2016 and 2017 the number of gender surgeries for natal females in the US quadrupled, with biological women suddenly accounting for—as we have seen—70 percent of all gender surgeries. In 2018, the UK reported a 4,400 percent rise over the previous decade in teenage girls seeking gender treatments. In Canada, Sweden, Finland, and the UK,

clinicians and gender therapists began reporting a sudden and dramatic shift in the demographics of those presenting with gender dysphoria—from predominately preschool-aged boys to predominately adolescent girls.[3]

Those stats are absolutely heartbreaking and alarming. Shrier goes on to say,

> While all this sexual identity politics marches through the front door, a large-scale robbery is taking place: the theft of women's achievement. The more incredible a woman is, the more barriers she busts through, the more "gender nonconforming" she is deemed to be. In this perverse schema, by definition, the more amazing a woman is, the less she counts as a woman.[4]

She is right. Women are being robbed of so much due to this transgender craze happening in our world. Not to mention, the very essence and beauty of our female biology is being diminished and degraded with terms like *people who menstruate* and *chestfeeding people*.

The two of us refuse to stand by and watch God's design for womanhood be crushed under this new wave of the sexual revolution. Absolutely not. If men can become women, then what is being a woman all about? We're here to expose the heartbreaking disorder of the trans movement and ensure that the beauty of God's design for women is upheld in the way He designed.

From Man to Woman to FAME

He was born a male and had dreams of being a famous actor. Unfortunately, those dreams were met with one closed door after another. Fame just didn't seem to be in his deck of cards. That is, until this full-grown man (with facial hair and the obvious anatomy of a male) took to the internet to share his story of becoming a girl. Yes, a girl. He wanted to be a little girl prancing around the world as if it was the most normal thing you'd ever seen.

The internet fell in love with this man and became obsessed with his videos. Chants and cheers of praise followed him wherever he went. He started the hormones, wore the over-the-top makeup, dressed in girls' clothing, and strutted around in the highest heels he could find. He was dressed like a she and the world fell in love with him.

His story of fame inspired thousands of other men and women to begin their transition and share their stories in hopes of finding fame as well. Why be an average man when you can dress up like a woman and receive praise and accolades from the world around you?

Move over, biologically born women. The men are here to show you how real womanhood is done. Talk about mansplaining at its finest.

Although the two of us disagree with the different waves of feminism on many levels, we can't help but wonder what some of the founders of the original movements would have thought about men intruding in women's spaces. These feminist leaders were fighting *for* women. Would they have been okay stepping aside to let biological men become some of the most famous "women" in the world? Would they have been on board with crowning a man as Woman of the Year? Would they have been okay with men claiming gold in women's sports?

Again, if nothing makes women unique, then what are feminists even fighting for?

> **If women can become men,
> then what makes men unique?**
>
> **If men can become women,
> then what makes women unique?**

In our modern day, it seems like the inner person is being elevated and the body is being diminished. It's all about who a person thinks and believes he or she is. You may have heard people say things like "What I feel is what I am" or "Who I believe I am is the truth of who I am." This mind-body split is something Nancy Pearcey discusses extensively in her excellent book *Love Thy Body*. In an interview about the book, Pearcey says, "The split between body and mind is even easier to recognize in the transgender narrative. According to a BBC documentary, at the heart of the debate is the idea that your mind can be 'at war with your body.' And in that war, the mind wins. What counts is not your biological sex but solely your feelings, desires, and sense of self."[5]

This mind-body split has taken us to some baffling places in our society. Just last night I (Bethany) saw a video on social media of a mom sharing her frustration that her local veterinarian would not see her son as a patient. You may be wondering why a loving mother would take her son to a vet and not a pediatrician. She said that her son identifies as a cat (identifying as an animal is actually considered a "queer identity," making this a crucial part of the trans conversation). She said that if he says he's a cat, then he's a cat and should be respected as such. She expressed frustration that the veterinarian wouldn't see him and that we have a long way to go toward equality in our world. We acknowledge that this story is satirical, but this is where this mind-body split sort of thinking takes us.

If the mind determines reality, then anything goes. If "my truth" determines truth, then anything can be true. There are entire communities of people called "furries" who live as pets or animals and get some sort of kink from living this way. There are entire communities of people who live as babies and again get some sort of kink out of this playacting.

While much of the mind-over-body perspective happening in our world is ridiculous (people are not cats, no matter how many collars you put on them), there are people genuinely struggling with what is medically called "gender dysphoria." The two of us have no doubt that many people actually do struggle with varying levels of gender dysphoria. We've had friends over the years who have shared their stories with us. The Mayo Clinic explains gender dysphoria this way: "Gender dysphoria is the feeling of discomfort or distress that might occur in people whose gender identity differs from their sex assigned at birth."[6]

I (Kristen) recently read a woman's story about her transitioning into manhood. She lived the majority of her life as a very successful career woman. Not to mention, she was also a wife and mom. She appeared to have everything a woman could want. Except happiness. She was deeply lost and lonely on the inside. All the material success only felt like a Band-Aid on her gaping wound of emptiness. This woman felt she was born in the wrong body. She suffered from what the world calls "gender dysphoria." Her answer to this inner struggle was to have her breasts removed and a fake penis constructed and to dress and present as a man. She changed her name and now lives as a male. This is the world's answer to gender dysphoria. This is what happens when you are the highest power in your life. This is what happens when your body has no deeper meaning about your God-given identity and your mind rules supreme.

Removing or replacing body parts is not the answer to gender dysphoria. There is a great article by Andrew T. Walker titled "The Transgender Fantasy: What I Wish Every Pastor Knew." In it, he says, "Hormones or surgery cannot override the underlying realities of our genetic structure. If culture tries to define male and female apart from anatomy and reproductive organization, male and female become fluid, absurd categories. Hence where we are as a culture."[7] The underlying realities of our genetic makeup should inform us of who God designed us to be. The very DNA and chromosomal structure of your body informs you of your identity as a male or female. Although your mind may feel confused at times, your God-assigned sex informs you of your reality. Men and women struggling with gender dysphoria do not have to live in confusion or wonder if God made a mistake. God never makes mistakes. Not with you and not with anyone else. It may sound too simplistic to say, "You need to align your mind with your body," but that's the reality of what we all need to do.

> Removing or replacing body parts is not the *answer* to gender dysphoria.

Does Transgenderism Exist?

A few years ago, I (Bethany) had the opportunity to do a social media paid collaboration with a megabrand. It was a huge opportunity for me to get paid, enjoy free products, and expose my community to this company. I received the product in the mail and began filming my content for my account. My content-posting day arrived and everything went live. The day seemed to be going great. I was happy and the company was happy. A few hours went by, and things took a turn for the worse.

There is an online community that strongly dislikes Girl Defined and the biblical principles we stand for. This online group has made it their mission to ruin any paid social media collaborations or sponsorships that we're involved in. This online group began flooding the DMs, comments, and email inboxes of the brand I was partnering with. They wanted this brand to know that they had partnered with one of the biggest transphobes on the internet and urged them to cut ties with me immediately. The brand I'd partnered with knew I was a Christian when I signed the contract. I'd seen them partner with other Christian women I follow as well. I assumed they'd just ignore the messages and move on with their day.

But that's the opposite of what they did.

I got an email with very vague terminology asking me to please remove all of my content because they were "going in a different direction." I knew the truth of why they wanted to cut ties with me, though. I responded by letting them know that my content was doing well and I was going to keep it up. That's when the call came in. They reached out to me directly and gave me an ultimatum: Remove my content by the end of the day or they would bring legal action against me. They called me with the threat and then followed up by email. They also made it clear that if I used their name or spoke disparagingly about them, they would sue as well (per my contract, they said).

Unfortunately, I had to remove the content and pretend like nothing happened. Nothing may have appeared to happen on the outside, but I was faced with a decision on the inside. Would I stop talking about God's design for gender in order to secure future collaborations? Would I soften my stance on biblical issues to ensure I could get paid social media sponsorships in the future? The answer was clear to me. I refuse to pretend that men can be women and women can be men. God's good design for gender is too important for me to remain silent about it. God's glory reflected in His image bearers is too valuable.

The two of us are more confident than ever that transgenderism does not exist. Walker points out, "Actual transgenderism does not exist. Sure, there are people who may have genuine confusion over their 'gender identity' (a concept itself riddled with problems), but the idea that there are persons truly 'trapped' in the wrong body is false. Scripture does not allow for such a dualism between the body and the 'self.'"[8] And that's where this conversation on the trans movement starts and ends. With Scripture. With God. With the Creator of humanity. With His good design for us. It doesn't matter what anyone else says about gender. God's Word is final because He is our good Designer. And we know that the only one who can define us is the One who designed us.

We discussed the creation of male and female in the previous chapters. It's clear from Genesis to Revelation that God designed the man and the woman. There is no room for gender fluidity or transgenderism in the full story of Scripture. A website the two of us frequent for biblical guidance

and direction is GotQuestions.org. They address the issue
this way:

> The Bible nowhere explicitly mentions transgenderism or
> describes anyone as having transgender feelings. However,
> the Bible has plenty to say about human sexuality. Most basic
> to our understanding of gender is that God created two (and
> only two) genders: 'male and female He created them' (Gen.
> 1:27). All the modern-day speculation about numerous gen-
> ders or gender fluidity—or even a gender 'continuum' with
> unlimited genders—is foreign to the Bible.[9]

The more we push against God's good design, the more
confusion and chaos follow. God is good, and His design for
His creation is good. And at the end of the day, life isn't about
human happiness. It's about being in an intimate relationship with God and knowing and being known by Him. It's
not about finding one's "true self." It's
about humbling ourselves before Him
and saying, "Who did You design me
to be, and how can I live my life to fully
glorify You?" The story of Scripture
is about Jesus. It's not about us. True
satisfaction and pleasure are found in
the presence of God. Not in having
certain anatomy. Psalm 16:11 reminds us of this truth. "You
make known to me the path of life; in your presence there is
fullness of joy; at your right hand are pleasures forevermore."
It's God who knows the path to true life. In His presence is
where we will be one day in heaven, and that's when we will
experience that perfect satisfaction and pleasure.

> The more we push against God's good *design*, the more confusion and chaos follow.

Typical Mean Girls

"The judgment. The cringe. The hateful opinions. What a train wreck. Let people be themselves. Why is it your business? Typical mean girls."[10] This was a recent review left on our podcast, *The Girl Defined Show*. If you're not already a listener, you need to be. We discuss all the hottest issues facing modern Christian women today. Thousands of women love our podcast, and thousands . . . well . . . don't love it. Comments like this one are often referring to our strong stance on biblical manhood, womanhood, sexuality, and gender distinctions. It can be hard to stand firm on biblical truth when you get name-called and told you're being a "mean girl" for those beliefs.

We have to remember what's at stake, though. God created each one of us on purpose and for a good purpose. For our flourishing and His glory. We (Kristen and Bethany) want the best for others, and that can only be found when they embrace their identity within God's design for them.

The two of us might be on the wrong side of history right now, but it has largely been the cultural norm and understanding that men are men and women are women. Somehow the modern transgender movement has overtaken these norms and convinced people that human sexuality has been wrong for millennia. It's a bold belief to think that this modern generation has finally figured out sexuality and gender. Albert Mohler, theologian and president of Southern Baptist Theological Seminary, writes,

> The Bible reveals that any attempt to subvert creation ends in disaster, not in human liberation. Our society stands on

the brink of that disaster. The great question remaining is whether there is enough sanity and courage left in our society to avoid the total abdication of truth. It is now plain to see that we face a demand to jump into the deep end of a pool of mass delusion. Whatever it takes, summon the courage to resist that dive.[11]

You might be called a mean girl for standing on biblical truth. We need more women who are willing to fearlessly say, "I was made by God to be she, and nothing can change that." It's not about being "right" or wishing ill on people. It's about praying for their best and knowing the only way for them to experience that is by submitting to the Creator.

There will always be men trying to become women and protesting at Christian conferences. There will always be women removing their breasts and dressing up as men. We can't stop that. But we can lovingly speak the truth of God's Word and say that God didn't make a mistake when He created humans. He didn't make a mistake when He gave you a female body. Allow your physical biology to speak to your God-given identity.

Chapter 8 Study Guide

"True satisfaction and pleasure are found in the presence of God. Not in having certain anatomy."

1. Fill in the blanks to this foundational statement about gender, which you read in this chapter: "The reason this topic matters so much is because _____ has become a _____ on God's good design for _____."

2. Why is the mind-body split worldview so problematic?

   _____

   _____

3. Can surgery and hormones fix the truest identity longings of a person's heart? Why or why not?

   _____

   _____

4. Where does this conversation on the trans movement start and end?

   _____

   _____

5. How can you stand firm on the truth of God's Word while still showing love toward those struggling with their gender?

_____

_____

6. Finish these statements:

"Biological men cannot become _____."

"Biological women cannot become _____."

chapter 9

Falling for the Birth Control Pill

She was born in 1879 to a sickly mother and a cruel father. Her parents had eleven children, and she was in the middle as the sixth born. Her father took every opportunity to physically beat the sons and to treat the daughters as he would slaves. He viewed his children more like objects than human beings. You can imagine the fear this young woman and her siblings must have experienced on a regular basis. Fear of abuse. Fear of neglect. And fear of the future. This young woman's life was full of dysfunction from the moment she was born.

Unfortunately, the heartache and pain only continued.

Her mother's health had been rapidly declining from the constant physical, emotional, and mental suffering. Her body finally had enough, and she was taken by tuberculosis.

It's said that this young woman looked across her mother's coffin at her father and yelled, "You caused this. Mother is dead from having too many children."[1] In that moment of anger and grief, something must have changed inside of this young woman. This grieving girl would grow up to become one of the most influential feminist saints ever to exist.

This woman was none other than Margaret Sanger.

She would eventually become the founder of the American Birth Control League, which would later become the multi-billion-dollar organization known as Planned Parenthood.

Margaret Sanger is held up by feminists as a hero and a saint.

This woman is most known for pouring her life into making birth control available to all women, thus changing the course of their futures. But few people are willing to pause and consider the dark side of this woman's background and beliefs.

So we will do that today.

Growing up, Margaret despised her large family and poor lifestyle. Something she was determined to avoid in her own future. Smaller families equaled wealth and happiness in her mind.

Margaret grew up and met a young man named William Sanger. She married him in 1902. He gave her much of what her materialistic heart desired. He showered her with gifts and long vacations. Still, Margaret found herself restless and unhappy.

She went on to have three children, hoping that the joy of motherhood would satisfy. It did not. Sadly, her own children were often farmed out to other families so that Margaret could pursue all her socialist and radical political ideals. Still, she was miserable. Her husband noticed her unhappiness and doted on her even more. But nothing seemed to satisfy her. It appears as though Margaret and William also had a difference of opinion on her attending orgies and having sex with other men. Something William didn't approve of her doing while she was married to him. Margaret decided enough was enough and left her husband. She was done with her marriage. She would look elsewhere for happiness.

This divorce really marked a turning point in Margaret's life trajectory. It's from this point forward that we start to see the crass, indecent, and sexually obsessed woman come to life. In a periodical titled *The Woman Rebel*, we get a glimpse inside Margaret's ever-growing belief system. Dr. George Grant, a pastor and prolific author, shares snippets of the monthly paper from his perspective and says, "The first issue denounced marriage as 'a degenerate institution,' capitalism as 'indecent exploitation,' and sexual modesty as 'obscene prudery.' In the next issue, an article entitled, 'A Woman's Duty' proclaimed that 'rebel women' were to 'look the whole world in the face with a go-to-hell look in the eyes.'"[2]

This is only the start of the wild remarks by the founder of Planned Parenthood. She was determined to change the minds of women, whatever the cost.

Her paper continued to be filled with crude ideas on what sexual liberation looked like. Women were challenged to leave behind all constraints of things like modesty, marriage, motherhood, commitment, and anything else that would hold them back. Full autonomy and sexual liberation was the goal.

Margaret's papers became so indecent that she was actually subpoenaed and indicted on three counts of the publication of lewd articles. To avoid prosecution, Margaret fled the country with a fake identity forged for her by her socialist friends. On her way out of the country, she left a final "in your face" to the government. She had one hundred thousand copies of her paper *Family Limitation* printed and distributed. "It was lurid and lascivious, designed to enrage postal authorities and titillate the masses. But worse, it was dangerously inaccurate, recommending things such as 'Lyson douches,' 'bichloride of mercury elixirs,' 'heavy doses of laxatives' and 'herbal abortifacients,' Margaret Sanger's dubious career as the 'champion of birth control' and 'patron saint of feminism' was well underway."[3]

Full autonomy and sexual *liberation* was the goal.

While in England fleeing prosecution, Margaret's lifestyle became even more obscene. Her bed had a constant rotation of men coming and going. She was deep in the free-love movement. She was using her life to show women what true liberation was all about. Under the mentorship of Havelock Ellis, a lover of sorts, she was exposed to a more exotic sexual lifestyle. She praised his radical political ideas and worshiped his unusual bedroom behavior. She even considered him to be a modern-day saint.

Margaret and Havelock devised a plan for her to return to the States after her yearlong hiatus in England ended. They schemed up a brilliant public relations campaign to explode the popularity of Margaret's reputation among the people in New York and beyond. Their strategy worked. The authorities were forced to drop all charges against Margaret due to her wild popularity and acceptance among her fellow Americans.

Margaret began traveling the country, drawing large crowds, speaking on topics like sex, marriage, birth control, abortion, and eugenics. She also went on to write her very first full-length book, which became an instant bestseller. Inside her book *The Pivot of Civilization*, "Margaret unashamedly called for the elimination of 'human weeds,' for the 'cessation of charity,' for the segregation of 'morons, misfits, and the maladjusted,' and for the sterilization of 'genetically inferior races.'"[4] She went on to say things like "the most urgent problem today is how to limit and discourage the over-fertility of the mentally and physically defective."[5] She surrounded herself with men and women who were fighting for eugenics, free love, and sexual promiscuity.

Margaret believed the world would be better off without the mentally or physically disabled. She believed in removing the "weeds" out of the world in a scientific way. And she believed this could be accomplished by the use of birth control, sterilization, and abortion.

This "feminist saint" and founder of Planned Parenthood was after a radicalization of the world. Birth control and abortion were necessities in order for the "morons" to be eliminated and for women to be sexually wild without constraint.

Despite Margaret's continued wild and free lifestyle, the huge success of her organization, Planned Parenthood, and the massive amounts of funding it received, she never seemed to find what she was truly looking for. Margaret Sanger passed away on September 6, 1966, a very bitter and depressed woman. It seems all the money, sex, freedom, and promiscuity didn't bring her the soul-satisfying liberation she deeply longed for.

Margaret's death didn't end her radical ideology, though. Her anti-God, anti-marriage, and anti-child legacy lives on.

To this day, Planned Parenthood has the biggest cultural influence on women regarding sex, marriage, and family. The birth control pill has had a worldwide impact, radically changing a woman's view of her sexuality. The promiscuous lifestyle that Margaret Sanger pioneered is now common to the average college-aged woman.

Margaret's work to legalize the birth control pill gave women the ability to embrace the wild, child-free lifestyle that she so loved.

Women no longer have to worry about things like commitment, marriage, or family. They can have sex whenever, wherever, and with whomever they want. The playing field between men and women has finally been "leveled." Women are now able to pursue a future without the constraints of their reproduction in play.

The Pill That Freed Women from Reproduction

The majority of us have no concept of what life was like before the pill. But if we rewind to the 1960s, we will get a glimpse of the impact the legalization of this drug had on women. Tim Harford, columnist for the British Broadcasting Corporation, describes the issue this way:

> The pill was first approved in the United States in 1960. In just five years, almost half of married women on birth control were using it.

But the real revolution would come when unmarried women got access to oral contraceptives. That took time. But in around 1970—10 years after the pill was first approved—US state after US state started to make it easier for single women to get the pill.

Universities opened family planning centers. By the mid-1970s, the pill was overwhelmingly the most popular form of contraception for 18 and 19-year-old women in the US.[6]

This shift in culture was monumental at the time.

Single women went from having to consider pregnancy as a possible outcome of sex to being able to have sex whenever and with whomever they wanted. Young women in their teens could now throw off their religious upbringings and jump into the sexually free lifestyle with no perceived consequences. Not to mention women could now delay childbearing and focus on building a career instead. Marriage and family were no longer the next logical steps for women. Careers could finally come first. Women were able to put biology aside and be just like men. Harford goes on to say, "A careful statistical study by the Harvard economists Claudia Goldin and Lawrence Katz strongly suggests that the pill must have played a major role in allowing women to delay marriage and motherhood, and invest in their own careers."[7]

The average age at which a woman got married in 1960 was 20.3. Compare that to the modern-day average age at which a woman gets married, which is 28.6.[8] When we take a look at childbearing, we see a similar statistic. In 1960, the average American woman had 3.66 children. Fast-forward to today, and the average American woman has just 1.66 children.[9]

Women have been told over and over again that equality with men means sameness. That means getting out of the home and into the workforce. That means taking a pill to avoid motherhood. That means having sex and delaying marriage. When you think about it, this is the very lifestyle that Margaret Sanger was fighting for. Complete control over one's life.

We, as women, did not end up here by accident. The obsession with total autonomy and control was the work of Margaret Sanger and many other feminist activists. But, as we've already discussed, women are not happier as a result. We're more depressed than ever before. Autonomy and control have not produced the deep satisfaction that we long for.

Just because something has become normalized (over 80 percent of fertile-aged women are taking oral contraceptives[10]), we shouldn't accept it as best for us.

A woman's biology is not an accident.

A woman's reproduction is not a curse.

A woman's nurturing nature is not something to diminish.

A woman's desire to connect deeply with the person she's sexually active with is not an accident.

A woman's growing baby in her womb is not someone to get rid of.

While the world around us continues to applaud the advancement of women's equality, we have to consider if this equality is what we actually want. Do we actually want to suppress our biological nature? Do we actually want to pursue a career over motherhood? Do we actually want to fight with men in the workforce? Do we actually want to let men off the hook from marriage and family? Let's be real. Men aren't suffering as a result of women's "equality." Men are no longer expected to step it up and care for women and children. Men are no longer expected to provide. Men are no longer expected to commit. Men are no longer expected to be strong and protective.

Women are now totally autonomous, and men are freed from familial responsibility. Just as women fought for it to be. And men aren't the ones hurting here. Women are.

The God of Modern Feminism

The two of us actually went back and forth on whether a chapter on the birth control pill, reproductive rights, and abortion should even be included in this book. We wondered if these were relevant enough topics to modern Christian women. It took only some preliminary research to convince us that a chapter on reproduction was an absolute must. We understand that not every woman on the birth control pill is taking it for pregnancy prevention. There are health reasons a woman might be on the pill. We acknowledge that. The focus of this chapter is to bring to light the massive impact pregnancy prevention (in the form of the birth control pill) has had on women around the world.

What Margaret Sanger started was only the beginning. Radical feminists are continuing to fight tooth and nail to take the work of their "saint" and spread it far and wide. They are doing everything in their power to convince women that their ability to get pregnant and nourish life is a curse rather than a blessing. They are working overtime to normalize a pregnant woman heading to a clinic to abort (murder) her baby. It's no big deal, women are told.

In fact, thousands of self-proclaimed feminists take to the streets every single year to rise up and shout their progressive feminist worldview with society. I (Bethany) looked at pictures from the most recent DC Women's March, and here are the phrases I saw on the majority of the banners and signs the women held:

"Rise Up for Reproductive Justice"
"Free Abortion On Demand"
"Women Demand Equality"
"Our Bodies. Our Abortions."

The annual Women's March places this as one of their top priorities: freeing women from their natural reproductive abilities through abortion. This truly has become the god of the modern feminist movement. And it seems to be the one thing left that truly unites all feminists.

One particular feminist gained national attention when her stand-up comedy special, in which she made jokes about the fact that she's had three abortions, went viral. Glamorizing things like "the childless lifestyle" and "abortion on demand" has become her mission. Since when did celebrities feel it necessary to romanticize total autonomy from family and kids with such satire?

Matt Wilstein, a West Coast–based senior editor overseeing The Daily Beast's entertainment news coverage, describes the comedy bit this way:

[She] made sure viewers knew she was speaking from experience as someone who had three abortions while still in high school. "And if that sounds too extreme, let's pretend I had two," she joked.

"Because here's the thing, this planet is a much safer place without me polluting it with my children," she concluded.[11]

This is the lifestyle feminism has built for us. A world where famous Hollywood stars use the murder of their preborn babies as laughing points for their comedy specials. It's stomach turning. One just has to pray that this woman comes to understand the full context of what she's saying and turns to God for grace and forgiveness.

Keep God out of My Uterus

I (Bethany) recently saw a sticker for sale online that featured a drawing of a nude woman sitting cross-legged with both her middle fingers up. She had these words written on her body: "My uterus. My business. My body. My choice." The message is loud and clear: *Back off and don't tell me what to do with my body*. The women who buy these stickers often want total control over their bodies. They do not want anyone (including God) to have a say in how they should live, the choices they make, or anything pertaining to their bodies.

This line of thinking makes sense if you reject God as Creator and view yourself as the final authority in your life: *You are your own god. You are the ruler of your body*. It makes sense that you wouldn't want anyone to tell you what to do with your body.

Unfortunately, thinking and believing something doesn't make it true. Even if you reject God and give Him the middle finger, He's still God. Even if you reject that God has authority over your uterus, He still has authority over your uterus. God created women. He created the uterus. He created sex. He created women to get pregnant. He designed babies to pull DNA from both parents, which creates their own unique genetic makeup. It was all His idea. It was all His design. That means He gets to decide what's right and wrong and the proper order and usage of His design.

Four Ways to View Your Reproduction as a Christian Woman

God should never be left out of the conversation when it comes to women and their biology. He should be at the center of that conversation. We should always be asking if the mindset and ideology we're embracing are in line with His design. We should always look to Him for wisdom. And we should always filter our confusion and questions through the lens of Scripture.

Here are four ways to view your reproduction in a God-honoring way:

1. Accepting God's Order for Marriage, Sex, and Baby Making

Sex isn't some erotic pleasure that Hollywood invented. God created it. The old children's rhyme had it right: *First comes love. Then comes marriage. Then comes the baby in the baby carriage.* Did you catch the order? This isn't by accident. God created attraction, and that's a good thing. That sexual attraction drives couples toward commitment. Toward marriage. It's only within that covenant that we see sexual intimacy celebrated in Scripture. God knew that things would get messy if people started having sex outside of marriage. That's why He designed sex for marriage and babies to be born into families. When we try to assert control and do things our own way, life gets messy. Everyone suffers as a result. Instead of trying to control, let's choose to submit to God's order.

2. Acknowledging That Women Do Not Own Their Bodies

It's just not true. It's not your body. It's not your choice. I love how Leah Savas from *WORLD* magazine unpacks this concept:

> Not only does the woman not own the body of the unborn baby, but she also doesn't own her own body. Any act of rebellion against God, including the destruction of a fellow creature, doesn't show autonomy and self-sufficiency. Instead, it's evidence of slavery to sin—a slavery that leads to death. Christ alone, by his death on the cross to pay for sins, can free us from that slavery. Even then, our bodies are not our own. "You are not your own, for you were bought with a price. So glorify God in your body," writes the Apostle Paul in 1 Corinthians 6. We find our fullness in Christ, who created us to glorify him in our bodies—not to glorify our own bodies, our own choices to the detriment of God's other lumps of clay.[12]

3. Realizing Your Two Middle Fingers Don't Make You the Queen

The heart posture of the Christian is not two middle fingers. It's one of humility. It's one that says, "Not my will, but yours, be done" (Luke 22:42). Surrender. Not control. We follow His plan for us even if we don't feel like it. We choose to say, "You are God, and I am not. I will follow You and trust You because You're my King. I surrender my control to You." Choose to follow His design for sex, marriage, and family. Ask for His will and not your own. And then take it a step further and boldly stand against the mockery of motherhood and against the abortion industry. Stand firm on the truth that God is the Giver of Life. We value life and motherhood because God does. We invite Him into our family planning because of our desire to do His will and not our own.

4. Inviting God into Your Fertility Journey

The majority of couples have the "When are we going to have kids?" conversation during engagement. Couples are often counseled to wait, and so most couples wait. The two of us rarely hear about a couple who says, "We're taking our family planning and family size to God. We're going to seek Him in this area of our lives. We're going to prayerfully approach this through a lens of Scripture and make a decision we believe is most honoring to God." That rarely happens. Most couples think, *Hmm . . . what do WE want?*

We're Christian women. Everything we do should be done with a heart posture of humility and a desire to seek God in the midst of it. Invite God into the center of your conversations about fertility and family planning. Instead of trying to control in this area, choose to submit to wherever He might lead. Family size and spacing between babies will look different for each couple, and that is why it's crucial to seek the Lord first and foremost.

What God Says about the Proper Use of Sex, Marriage, and Your Uterus

Sex was designed for the covenant of marriage. (Heb. 13:4; Song of Sol. 4)

Married couples are encouraged to bring forth children. (Gen. 1:28)

Children are a blessing and a heritage of a married couple. (Ps. 127:3–5)

All humans (from conception to death) are image bearers of God. (Gen. 1:26)

God knits a baby together in the womb. (Ps. 139:13–14)

You are not your own. You are God's. (1 Cor. 6:19–20)

Your body is a temple of the Holy Spirit. Honor God with your body. (1 Cor. 6:19–20)

At the end of the day, our life choices can be summed up in one big, scary word: *submission*. Will we submit to our Creator and to His design? Or will we reject His good design for us and instead do things our own way? God's design for marriage, sex, and family isn't meant to be a punishment. It's actually the opposite. It's meant to help us live flourishing lives and keep the world flourishing as well.

When you submit to God, you're essentially echoing the words of 1 Corinthians 6:19–20: "Or do you not know that your body is a temple of the Holy Spirit within you, whom you have from God? You are not your own, for you were bought with a price. So glorify God in your body." This is what it means to be a Christian. Acknowledging that God is God and we are not. This is why reproduction matters so much. This is why the two of us care about your perspective on reproduction so much. We care about women's reproduction because God cares about it. We care about marriage because God cares. We care about sex because God cares about it. We care about women's designed biological nature because God cares.

We're Done Being Pitted against Our Reproduction

I (Bethany) remember being strongly encouraged to visit my OB-GYN before getting married. There were several older couples leading the church's premarital class for us younger couples, and visiting the OB was brought up several times. I finally built up the courage and raised my hand. I asked the ladies why I needed to see the doctor before getting married.

Their answer was simple: to get on the birth control pill.

I was surprised that getting on the pill was the blanket advice they gave to all of us. While I do not see any direct commands in Scripture against family planning or waiting to start having babies, I do believe every couple should seek the Lord for His will for their family size. Having conversations and education around family planning can be so beneficial to young couples.

Understanding the science behind the natural family-planning method can be a great alternative to taking oral contraceptives.

Understanding the health risks of taking hormonal birth control is important for every woman.

Understanding the pros and cons of starting or delaying motherhood is something every woman should think through.

Understanding what God has to say in the area of family planning is a must in order to make a godly decision.

And seeking the Word to see what God has to say about having kids, and the blessing they are, is crucial as we consider the legacy we want to leave.

We, as Christian women, must view our reproduction and fertility through the lens of Scripture. We must seek God in this area of our lives. We must choose to submit to what He wants for our families.

The radical feminists who fought for birth control and abortion value the exact opposite of what God values. That should cause us to pause and consider if blindly following their path is best for our flourishing and God's glory.

Chapter 9 Study Guide

"God should never be left out of the conversation when it comes to women and their biology. He should be at the center of that conversation."

1. How does Margaret Sanger's life still impact women today?

2. Finish these statements:

   Your biology is not an _____.

   Your reproduction is not a _____.

   Your nurturing nature is not something to _____.

   Your desire to connect deeply with the person you're sexually active with is not an _____.

3. What is wrong with the following message?

   "My uterus. My business. My body. My choice."

4. Write down the four ways you should view your reproduction as a Christian woman:

   a.

   b.

   c.

   d.

5. What would it look like for a woman to submit her reproduction to God?

_____

_____

6. Look up 1 Corinthians 6:19–20 and write down how you should view your life through this lens.

_____

_____

chapter 10

Trading In Motherhood for a Career

I t had been a long day of chasing little kids around, and I (Kristen) was exhausted. We started off the day by going to the zoo, then we ate lunch at a nearby park. Next, we went home, where I cleaned up the house while the kids took an oh-so-quick thirty-minute nap. That was followed by playing Legos on the floor for an hour, then reading books for a while. And finally, we finished off the day by going on a long walk with the double stroller. It was a good but tiring day.

These boys were sweet, and I loved spending time with them. But they weren't my kids. I was in my early twenties at the time and had been hired as their full-time nanny. The sweet Christian couple who brought me on needed someone to care for their kids while they both worked demanding, full-time jobs.

Even though I left each day feeling exhausted, I enjoyed my time with those two adorable little boys. Whenever we went out somewhere, I would get nonstop compliments on how adorable "my" kids were. Sometimes I would tell people they weren't mine . . . and other times I would just smile.

As the weeks and months went by, I grew to love those little boys. I guess that makes sense because I was spending the majority of my time with them. I would arrive at their house just before 8:00 a.m. and wouldn't leave until close to 6:00 p.m. They went to bed at 7:30 p.m., so most of their waking hours were spent with me.

As much as I loved my job, I couldn't help but feel a twinge of sadness for how much time they didn't get with their own parents. As I watched them take their first steps, say their first words, and kick their first soccer ball, I wondered if their mama was sad that she couldn't be there for those moments. I knew she worked hard in her career and was passionate about her work, but I also wondered if she realized how much she was missing.

One afternoon while I was at the house with the boys, I looked up to see that the younger of the two boys had pulled over a little chair and was sitting right under what I called "the accomplishment wall." This was the wall in their house that featured all of their parents' academic accomplishments. Lined with numerous diplomas from Ivy League schools, top performing awards, and certificates of achievement, this wall made it very clear—whoever lived here was highly successful.

Not wanting to miss out on the fun, the older brother found another little chair and dragged it over to the wall. Sitting side by side and looking quite proud of what they had done, both boys looked up at me and smiled. My heart melted. They were adorable. But the sight in front of me caused a lump to form in my throat. For all the accomplishments and success that their parents had achieved, they were missing out on the most precious gift of all.

I wondered if the cost was truly worth it.

Us versus Them

The topics of motherhood and work are ones that often feel controversial and combative within women's circles. As Christian women, we have a tendency to adopt an "us versus them" mindset depending on the perspective we're personally coming from. There are the "stay-at-home mom versus working mom" debates, right? We get that. However, this chapter isn't for one group of women . . . but for all of us. Because here's the deal: God created women with the unique ability to give birth and become moms, but He also created us to work hard. As we'll unpack in this chapter, the Proverbs 31 woman was highly industrious and entrepreneurial within her home and outside her home. But as we'll also see, her heart was not driven by a prideful determination to make something of herself; rather, she humbly desired to work hard for the good and flourishing of her family. *Serving others* was a core driver for her. She exemplified the same heart attitude that our own Savior modeled. "For even the Son of Man came not to be served but to serve" (Mark 10:45).

> God created women with the unique *ability* to give birth and become moms, but He also created us to *work* hard.

Regardless of whether you're single or married, have kids or don't, our prayer is that this chapter will help you see the beauty of God's design for motherhood and work in fresh, gospel-centered ways. That we would each humbly seek to become wise women who build our homes for God's glory. As Proverbs 14:1 exhorts us, "The wisest of women builds her house, but folly with her own hands tears it down."

As we've explored in previous chapters, we must remember that we have an enemy who is seeking to destroy God's design for womanhood—*including motherhood*. Satan has been twisting and distorting God's plan from the beginning (starting in Gen. 3), weaving crafty deceptions in order to lead us astray. There is a bigger battle happening, which is why we desperately need God's Word and His Spirit to help us engage in this fight with wisdom and truth. We need the Holy Spirit's help to "take every thought captive to obey Christ" (2 Cor. 10:5). We need to ask God for humble hearts that are open to conviction with a willingness to follow Him wherever He leads us.

The Funnel for Female Success

Most of us don't even realize it's happening. But as young single women, we are conditioned by society to follow a very specific path for our lives. We might think we're spreading our wings and exercising our independence, but we're really just pawns in a repetitive cycle. From cultural influences and feminist ideology to peer pressure—each one of us is pushed toward the same funnel. We (Kristen and Bethany) endearingly call it "the funnel for female success." It's an unspoken path that millions of young women robotically travel down because it's *expected*. It's what's normal. And it looks something like this:

Age 18:

Leave home to pursue higher education.

Age 18–22:

Attend college.

Get on birth control (if you're not already).

Have multiple sexual partners.

Don't get pregnant.

Age 22:

Graduate college with thousands of dollars in debt.

Age 23:

Pursue a full-time career.

Age 24–29:

Work full-time.

Cohabitate.

Age 30–35:

Get married.

Have your first child.

Age 35–45:

Put your child/children in full-time daycare.

Continue building your career.

Brace for a 50 percent chance of divorce.

Age 45–65:

Continue climbing the ladder.

Retire and live the "good life."

This is the funnel for female success. Now, of course, every woman doesn't follow this exact trajectory. But have you noticed how many actually do? Maybe you've traveled partway down this funnel yourself. It's not that every single thing about this path is wrong. And we're not against women getting educated, nor do we think every form of working outside the home is wrong. But this path does have some major flaws. It pits women against their fertility. It forces young moms to choose between their career and their baby. It ignores a woman's reproductive years and downplays her biological clock. But most of all, it disregards God. It puts self at the center, encouraging a world-informed path over a Word-informed path. Proverbs 14:8 reminds us that "the wisdom of the prudent is to discern his way." This biblical wisdom can only come from being rooted in the Word and directed by His Spirit.

The two of us want to challenge the status quo and question what we've all accepted as normal. Many of us have jumped aboard this popular path, assuming it's for our good . . . but is it? Is it really landing women and families in a better place? Is it truly setting moms and babies up to thrive? Is it encouraging us, as Christian women, to pursue lives built on the wisdom of God's Word?

We don't think so. And we also don't believe this funnel came out of thin air. It's not a coincidence that millions of women follow it.

This funnel was curated for us. We've been groomed for it by the very feminist ideologies that seek to downplay the family and minimize motherhood. We've been deceived by our true enemy into believing the lie that motherhood isn't truly an ambitious pursuit for the successful woman. We've been taken captive by worldly ideas that fuel our pride and place self at the center.

I'm *Just a Mom*

Our table was covered with piles of paper. We were refinancing our house, and our signatures were needed on everything. I (Kristen) reached for another stack. *Maybe this is what it feels like to be a famous person signing autographs for fans.* It was exhausting work. I had more sympathy for them. Count your blessings, I guess.

As I began flipping through this new pile, I came to a section that asked for more than basic signatures. It needed to know everything about our personal lives and work. I began filling it out. Everything was smooth sailing until I got to a little section that said "occupation." It had one line for my husband and one line for me. I quickly filled out Zack's line but then paused on mine. I wasn't sure what to put. Tapping my pen on the table, I stared out the window in deep thought.

"Stuck on something?" Zack asked, snapping me back to reality.

"Yeah, I'm just trying to figure out what to put down for my occupation," I responded.

"Oh," Zack said, looking confused. "Um . . . how about stay-at-home mom?"

I scrunched my nose in distaste. "I don't know . . . maybe."

I didn't say it out loud, but in that moment, the phrase *stay-at-home mom* sounded so lame to me. It sounded so unsuccessful. I wanted to appear more "ambitious" on this paper.

"Um . . . how about author and writer?" I offered back with a questioning look.

"Yeah, sure. Fine with me," Zack said indifferently, moving to another stack of papers.

My pen tapped the table some more.

Biting my lower lip, I stared down at that little black line. Why did I care so much about what my occupation was on this stupid paper? Some random person at the mortgage company was the only one who would see this. Yes, I was a stay-at-home mom. And I loved it. But I was also many other things . . . and those things seemed more impressive and ambitious at that moment.

Lifting my pen, I slowly wrote the words *author, writer, mom*.

Shoving that paper to the bottom of my stack, I robotically kept signing . . . but deep down, a nagging feeling wouldn't leave me alone.

Looking back on that moment now, I cringe at my inner struggle to embrace my title of stay-at-home mom. Even as someone who was literally writing books on biblical womanhood and cheering on godly femininity, I was struggling. That moment was eye-opening for me on a personal level. It revealed just how much I was falling prey to the same feminist lies about motherhood and success that entrap most women today. It revealed how much I was being deceived by the enemy into thinking that motherhood wasn't a valuable pursuit. It opened my eyes to the pride of my own heart and my inner desire for worldly approval and praise.

If you talk to any modern young woman graduating from high school, she will most likely tell you the many dreams and ambitions she has for her future. But there will almost always be one thing she will never mention in her list of plans. *Motherhood*. Although she will probably get married someday and will most likely become a mom . . . this will never be vocalized in her dreams. Why? Because feminism has ingrained the idea inside of us that motherhood is a lowly and unambitious career path. We're told that a woman can be anything she wants, as long as it's *outside* of homemaking. This messaging naturally appeals to our flesh because—let's face it—there is a lot more acclaim that comes with working outside of the home than inside. In our pride, we're naturally drawn toward what will make us *feel* most successful in the world's eyes.

The ditch of feminist womanhood traps us when we believe the lie that men and women *must* do the same kinds of work to be equal. For decades, feminists pushed the idea that true equality between men and women would be realized only when women got out of their homes and into the workforce. They demanded that 50 percent of every profession needed to be female.

> The ditch of feminist womanhood traps us when we *believe* the lie that men and women must do the same *kinds* of work to be equal.

In order to accomplish this monumental task of getting women out of their homes, they had to downplay, devalue, and degrade motherhood and homemaking altogether. This was strategically and systematically done.

Sharon James points out that "during the 1960s and 1970s a small number of highly vocal activists and academics wanted women to realize that marriage, motherhood, and homemaking were symptoms of female oppression, satisfying only for those who were mentally subnormal or emotionally weak."[1] Well-known feminists like Simone de Beauvoir and Betty Friedan published books highlighting the oppression of domesticity. They argued that women could not find true happiness or fulfillment within their homes. True meaning and liberation could be found only by entering the workforce. James goes on, "De Beauvoir believed there can only be genuine relationships between men and women when the woman is self-sufficient economically. The public world is significant. To be trapped at home is degrading. If women say that they are happy at home it means that they have been brainwashed. They need to be liberated, forcibly if necessary, from the family."[2]

As outrageous and offensive as many of these feminist claims were, they worked. Slowly but surely, housewives felt the pressure to make something of themselves. They began believing the lie that true female happiness could be achieved only by denying all biological realities and drives and forcing themselves (and their children) out of the home.

Before long, motherhood became the lowest priority on the female measurement for success. Over the next few decades, classes like home economics, among others, disappeared from public schools as young women were pushed toward more ambitious futures. A new generation of women emerged. And these women were passionately determined to become far more than "just moms."

Girl, You Can Have It *All*

"Freeze Your Eggs, Free Your Career." That was the eye-catching headline on the front page of a *Bloomberg Business-*

week magazine. The subheadline read, "A New Fertility Procedure Gives Women More Choices in the Quest to Have It All." My (Kristen's) interest was sparked. I scanned this intriguing story. "Later, Baby" was the title on the inside, with the headline "Egg Freezing Technology Is Helping Women Kiss the Mommy Track Goodbye."[3]

As I continued reading the article, I came across several stories of women who had decided to take the egg-freezing route, along with their reasons for doing so. "I just wanted to take the pressure off," Suzanne, age 37, said. "Men don't have a biological clock, and I felt like this leveled the playing field a bit."

The article continued, "Like many people who've frozen their eggs, Emily uses the word 'empowered' to describe the experience."

Essentially, this egg-freezing technology would allow women to surgically remove some of their eggs at a younger age, then freeze them in a lab to be used at a later date (maybe a decade or more later). Since a woman's fertility declines over time, this technology promised women freedom from their God-designed biological clock.

The article's main point was that women could finally have it all. Technology had advanced enough to allow women to overcome their biggest challenge: *biology.* With the birth control pill already widely accepted, women were conditioned to view their reproduction as something negative that needed to be overcome. While the birth control pill promised women sexual freedom and reproductive control, egg-freezing technology promised women complete biological autonomy.

Rather than viewing reproduction as a unique gift given to women by God, feminist activists reframed this to be a *disadvantage.* In their minds, a woman's fertility caused the playing field between men and women to be grossly unequal. Having babies wasn't a gift to be embraced but a hurdle to overcome.

But what about when a woman wants to have a baby? What would happen to her career then? This was the other "problem" feminist activists were trying to solve.

There wasn't enough time in the day for a truly ambitious woman to pursue her career full-time while also taking care of a needy baby full-time. And since motherhood was downgraded to little more than a childcare position, it made no sense for a successful woman to waste her time filling it. Feminist activists saw this dilemma and began pushing for a solution. The answer? *Universal childcare.* An article in *The Atlantic* stated that "the National Organization for Women actually called for free 24-hour child care for all."[4] Activists believed that in order to keep women financially independent of men, the state would need to step in as the primary caregiver. Women were calling on the government to raise their babies.

Although free universal childcare did not become a reality (praise the Lord), the idea of full-time daycare appealed to women. In the name of "having it all," young moms felt compelled to place their tiny little newborn babies in full-time institutionalized care. In their minds, this was the best option. After all, they had a pile of school debt to pay off and a future to prove. Never mind that some moms would secretly cry after dropping their newborns off at daycare— this was what empowered womanhood looked like. Just wipe off your dripping mascara and press on!

Feminist mantras and talking points were catchy, but as time went on, the reality of this lifestyle was anything but empowering for many moms. And it definitely wasn't empowering for their children. Research is now showing that daycare is no substitute for a mother's loving care for her baby. In fact, an article in *Salvo* magazine titled "Inconvenient Truths about Childcare Subvert the Very Best Intentions" reveals that full-time daycare can be damaging to a child's emotional development and ability to attach well.[5]

In her eye-opening book, *Doing Time: What It Really Means to Grow Up in Daycare*, May Saubier challenges parents to rethink the daycare system. In an article from the *National Review*, she says, "A day spent in daycare begins with abandonment. Staff members are prepared for this and employ many strategies to lessen the daily blow. A baby who spends five years at one center will lose one-third to almost half of her caregivers every twelve months or so. At any given moment, a parent's baby could be in the arms of someone they don't know well, or someone they have never met at all. Children in daycare are frequently cared for by strangers."[6]

In light of this reality, some moms are turned off by this form of care and instead turn to other options. Hiring a full-time nanny or even a live-in au pair became popular among wealthier families. Although this care has advantages (more one-on-one time and the ability for the child to stay home), it's still missing the most important element of all— the *mom*.

Even the loving care of a grandma, sister, or close friend isn't an equal substitute to the tender care of a baby's own *mother*.

For decades, we've been fed the lie that women *can* have it all. That we should have it all. Things like birth control, egg freezing, and full-time daycare tell us that motherhood isn't really all that important. Anyone can watch a baby. Don't waste your best years on *that*.

But what they don't add into the equation is the *trade-off*. Are women really gaining it *all*? Or are we actually losing the most important and precious things along the way?

Oh, Wait . . . a *Blessing*?

"Whatever you do, just don't have kids in your first year of marriage. In fact, wait a few years if you can." This was the advice that my husband and I (Bethany) received in a Christian class for engaged couples before we were married. The message was clear: Don't have kids too early or it will mess up your marriage.

Hmm.

Thanks, but no thanks. We didn't listen.

In my opinion, one of the most subtle yet damaging lies circulating in Christian and non-Christian circles is that children are a burden and something to be put off as long as possible. As women, we've been fed a steady diet of comments like:

"Don't have kids too early!"

"Just wait until you're much older."

"Enjoy life first before you take the plunge."

"Kids are so expensive!"

"Oh, you're pregnant? Congrats . . . just be prepared to lose your brains and your freedom!"

With so much negativity surrounding parenthood, no wonder couples are scared to start trying.

However, the message we see from the Bible is the polar opposite. When we look in Scripture, we see that God has a welcoming heart toward children. "Behold, children are a heritage from the LORD, the fruit of the womb a reward. Like arrows in the hand of a warrior are the children of one's youth" (Ps. 127:3–4). Jesus Himself welcomed little children when His own disciples tried to keep them away. "Let the little children come to me and do not hinder them, for to such belongs the kingdom of heaven" (Matt. 19:14). The Bible even highlights the generational blessing that children bring. "Grandchildren are the crown of the aged, and the glory of children is their fathers" (Prov. 17:6).

According to the Bible, children are a blessing, not a burden. They are not accessories to be tacked onto your life when it feels convenient. They are a literal heritage from the Lord. The word *heritage* speaks of something long term and lasting. So often, women get stuck on the challenges of the "baby phase" but forget about the reality of the bigger picture. Your child is a human being—an eternal soul that you have the privilege of nurturing and raising. That's an incredible heritage.

> Jesus Himself *welcomed* little children when His own disciples tried to keep them away.

Clearly, a biblical view of children sees them as a *blessing*. But sadly, thanks to the funnel for female success, women today are not set up to receive this blessing. This lifestyle track for the "successful feminist woman" is not hospitable to motherhood or the home. It doesn't make room for having babies. This is why so many young moms feel forced to place their newborns in daycare when the time comes. They have to choose between their career and their kids.

As Christian women seeking to honor God with our lives, we need to seriously rethink this funnel. As we're making plans for our future, we would be wise to consider how motherhood will fit in.

> ## We Should Take Time to Ask Ourselves Important Questions Like These:
>
> - Will this education and career path pit me against motherhood someday?
> - Is the path I'm considering hospitable to the family and the home?
> - As a mom, if I pursue this job outside the home, will I be able to disciple and care for my children as God calls me to?
> - If I choose to pursue this full-time career (whether working from home or not), will I be forced to pass off my children to someone else?

Now, we understand that not all moms will have the life circumstances that enable them to be with their kids as much as they desire. Our heart goes out to single moms raising their children alone. If you find yourself in that position, there is special grace from the Lord for you. Continually seek the Lord, and He will give you wisdom on how to navigate your circumstances for His glory.

We also know that not all women who desire children will be able to have them. We want you to know that your worth and purpose as God's daughter is not diminished by not having children. Even if you never have physical children on this earth, God is still calling you to be fruitful by raising up spiritual children through discipleship and mentoring. Your God-given design to nurture relationships and produce life can still be pursued in beautiful ways.

For the young woman not yet married, planning ahead is incredibly helpful in preparing your life to welcome children someday. Don't blindly follow the funnel for female success. Think about your future and plan your life in a way that reflects the fact that children are a *blessing*.

For the married woman who already has children, search your heart and evaluate your priorities. Ask the Lord to show you any areas of your life where your values don't align with His heart for children. Ask Him to deepen your love and commitment toward your children and home.

God Cares about Motherhood

The two of us went from no kids to four kids within two years. Between two home births (Bethany's) and the adoption of two boys (Kristen's), our lives changed really fast. As sisters, it was exciting to enter this new and wild season together. For years, we had been championing God's role of motherhood through Girl Defined Ministries . . . and now it was our turn to actually live it out.

Becoming moms has been one of the sweetest and most precious gifts of our lives. But we'll be totally honest with you here. It hasn't been easy. The daily rigors of motherhood are not for the faint of heart. We've had to change the way we do life and our Girl Defined ministry work. We've had to say no to many things in order to prioritize our children and our homes. We've had to constantly fight against the feminist lies about female success when our day feels like nothing more than a monotonous cycle of small tasks. We've had to regularly remind our own hearts that God deeply values children and motherhood and has called us into this important role. We've had to lean into God's grace and strength as we regularly realize we don't have what it takes (see 2 Cor. 12:9). We're not enough. *We need Him.*

We've also seen God use our children as a primary means of sanctifying *us*. The challenges we face on a daily basis reveal our need for Jesus in our lives. In our flesh, we get tired of serving and constantly pouring out for others. It can be exhausting. But then we're reminded of our Savior, who "came not to be served but to serve, and to give his life as a ransom for many" (Mark 10:45). Motherhood is a daily opportunity to show our kids the love and sacrifice of Christ through our love for them. It is a sanctifying and refining season that God wants to use to shape each of our hearts and lives to become more like Christ. As we depend on Him, we teach our kids to do the same.

Throughout this journey, we have also learned how deeply God cares about motherhood. He speaks directly to this area multiple times in the Bible. Passages like Titus 2:3–5 specifically command older women to teach young moms the importance of valuing their husbands, homes, and children:

Older women likewise are to . . . teach what is good, and *so train the young women* to love their husbands and children, to be self-controlled, pure, working at home, kind, and submissive to their own husbands, that the word of God may not be reviled. (emphasis added)

Of all the things older women could have been commanded to teach younger women, isn't it interesting how the emphasis is on her family, home, and character? It sounds like the young moms of that era were tempted to downplay and minimize their homes just like we are today.

Another passage that emphasizes God's heart for the home and family is Proverbs 31. This chapter paints a vivid picture of a hardworking woman who had her priorities straight (we encourage you to read the entire chapter on your own).

The Proverbs 31 mom had guts and gumption. She was a go-getter! This passage completely debunks the myth that homemakers are nothing more than boring doormats. Clearly, God is not calling women to leave their brains and skills at the entrance. This passage shows us the value of women being hard workers, entrepreneurs, intelligent, skillful, kind, intentional, trustworthy in marriage, and purposeful in prioritizing their children. Everything this woman does is for the good of her household. She works hard because she loves and fears the Lord. Her work is fueled by her worship. She pursues work inside and outside of her home in a way that blesses and prioritizes her family. While feminism encourages you to work hard for yourself, Proverbs 31 encourages you to work hard for the good of your family and for the glory of God.

This woman isn't a picture of *perfect* womanhood but of *purposeful* womanhood.

Your job as a Christian mother is to be present *so that* you can disciple your children in the ways of the Lord. Deuteronomy 6:7 calls parents to teach their children God's Word "when you sit in your house, and when you walk by the way, and when you lie down, and when you rise." Intentional Christian mothering has a purposeful focus on teaching your children about Jesus.

When it comes to being a godly wife and mother, there isn't a one-size-fits-all box. The Bible doesn't give us a detailed checklist. Instead, passages found in Genesis 2, Deuteronomy 6, Proverbs 31, and Titus 2 give us a vision of God's design and heart for women and motherhood.

Your life will be filled with many different stages, seasons, needs, and opportunities—choose to seek God's wisdom within each one for how to faithfully honor Him and prioritize your family.

Motherhood is a noble calling. It's a worthy career path. It's a successful pursuit. It is something worth prioritizing, planning for, and valuing. Regardless of our age, stage, or season of life, each one of us should be fearlessly championing a biblical view of *motherhood*.

Chapter 10 Study Guide

"Motherhood is a noble calling. It's a worthy career path. It's a successful pursuit. It is something worth prioritizing, planning for, and valuing."

1. How have you seen "the funnel for female success" at play in your life (or in the lives of women around you)?

2. Look at the scale below and circle the number that represents what has been most influential in shaping your view of motherhood:

The world   God's Word

1   2   3   4   5   6   7   8   9   10

Write down the three biggest factors (things/people) that have shaped your view.

a. _____

b. _____

c. _____

3. In what ways have you believed the feminist messaging that women can (and should) have it all?

4. Does your heart reflect God's heart and priority in viewing children as a blessing? Why or why not?

_____

_____

5. Take some time right now to prayerfully read each of the Scripture passages below, then write down any truths that you need God's help to embrace and walk faithfully in.

Deuteronomy 6:7 _____

_____

_____

Psalm 127:3–4 _____

_____

_____

Titus 2:3–5 _____

_____

_____

Proverbs 31:10–31 _____

_____

_____

chapter 11

Chasing Beauty at All Costs

Wearing tight pants and heavy makeup with my blonde hair straightened down my back, I (Kristen) confidently walked into the convention center. I was here for a modeling job. I had been contracted through my agency to work as a promo model for a particular vendor at this convention. I was in my early twenties and had been modeling for only a few months.

Becoming a model was something that had intrigued me for years. As a teen girl, I would regularly get approached by modeling recruiters while out in public, and they would hand me their business cards and try to convince me to come work for them. My parents never encouraged me toward this line of work because they knew the pitfalls of the industry. I was also busy with school, sports, and friends, so I didn't think much about it. But as I hit my early twenties, I wanted to try it for myself. I was enticed by the idea of getting paid simply for being glamorous and beautiful. I had sifted through the agency cards I'd been saving in my underwear drawer and come across the company that I now would be working for.

Glancing down at the paper in my hand, I made my way to their booth, where a middle-aged man was busily getting things ready. He looked up as I approached.

"Oh, you must be Kristen?" he asked with a pleased smile.

"Yes, nice to meet you," I responded as we shook hands.

"Okay, honey," he quickly began, staring straight at me. "Your job is to sit here behind the booth and draw customers in. That's it. No need to talk unless they talk to you. Just be my eye candy."

Feeling a little uncomfortable by the gleam in his eye, I took my seat. I didn't love the idea of sitting behind his booth all day as nothing more than an ornament . . . but that's what I was hired for. This was the job.

Shortly after the convention began, customers came flooding to his booth. I hoped my contribution was the reason. I smiled and tried hard to look deeply engaged as my eyes wandered to the booth across the aisle. Apparently that vendor had hired a model as well. She looked about my age and wore a tight T-shirt paired with a miniskirt. She had long, dark hair and generous curves. Flirting with the vendor employees and making intentional eye contact with every customer who walked up, she seemed to know what she was doing. I secretly wondered if I was as good or as pretty as her.

The man I was working for apparently noticed the same thing. Staring across the aisle, he leaned toward me and said, "Will you check her out? Wow. She's gorgeous." His eyes slowly moved up and down her body. "They really nailed it with her," he said, dramatically exhaling.

I affirmed his comment with a simple "yeah," but my thoughts quickly spiraled down into a place of jealousy, comparison, and discontentment. I looked nothing like this voluptuous bombshell. She was curvy and had long, dark, silky hair, sun-kissed skin, perfect legs, full lips, and well-defined facial features. My tall, lanky, less-curvy body, blonde hair, fair skin, and average-sized lips seemed to pale in comparison to her.

For the rest of the convention, I wondered if the man who hired me was secretly disappointed that he drew the "short stick."

You Are Ugly

When it comes to a woman's beauty and physical appearance, there's a subtle lie that entraps most of us. And it goes something like this: "You are ugly. You will only be beautiful and happy once you change _____."

Even as a model, I (Kristen) wasn't content with my outward appearance. It didn't matter that dozens of other people called me beautiful or that I carried the title of "model" for a while. I fell prey to the same lie that gets most women. Even at the peak of my youthfulness in my early twenties, I remember standing in front of my bedroom mirror and critiquing my nose and skin. Then I would turn around and critique my butt and legs. I would imagine how much happier and more beautiful I would be if I could only change those things.

The lie that we will be happy once we change _____ is a loop that never ends. No matter how much a woman changes her appearance to find beauty, she will never be satisfied. There will always be someone else who is prettier or has the one thing she doesn't. Even some of the most famous supermodels of our day have shared how the women in their industry are some of the unhappiest and most discontent with their appearance. And they're supermodels! Is there any hope for the rest of us?

A quick glance at history reveals the female obsession with beauty over the centuries.

In 1908, a small statue of a plump woman was found in Austria. Called the Venus of Willendorf, it's believed to be thousands of years old and is one of the earliest known portrayals of female beauty. With short legs, a pear-shaped body, and large breasts, she was considered the "ideal" for female beauty and fertility at that time. All the way into the seventeenth and eighteenth centuries, artists continued to portray the ideal woman as curvy and voluptuous.

In the nineteenth century, clothing styles and fashions evolved, shifting the ideal for women away from a pear-shaped look to one with a small waist and large curves. The corset was invented to help women achieve this look by forcing their bodies into this shape.

In the twentieth century, beauty standards took a dramatic shift. The ideal body moved away from curves and toward a slender, thinner frame. The rise of the 1920s flapper dress reflected this shift as the Western world desired a slimmer physique. In a CNN Health article on the history of female beauty, Jacqueline Howard says,

> As slender women's bodies started to appear in magazines in the mid-1920s, an epidemic of eating disorders also occurred among young women, according to some studies.

"The highest reported prevalence of disordered eating occurred during the 1920s and 1980s, the two periods during
which the 'ideal woman' was thinnest in US history."[1]

By the 1940s, slender body types went out of vogue as the
bust-to-waist ratio climbed up again. In the 1950s, celebrities like Marilyn Monroe and pinup models popularized the
hourglass body type again. Female beauty was curvy, sexy,
and well endowed. The first *Playboy* magazine was published
in 1953. A woman's body and sexuality became a commer-
cialized commodity on a mass scale for the first time.

In response to this, second-wave feminists of the 1960s
and '70s set out to reclaim the female body by pushing back
against "pinup" culture. As a result, the bust-to-waist ratio
reverted back to thinner body types as the ideal standard
for beauty changed once again. "People talk about the '60s,
even the '70s, as this moment when the woman's body is
freed," Howard noted. "But that notion that women were
all of a sudden completely free in their bodies after that
point is a complete fallacy."[2] Women were struggling to be
thin *enough*.

In the 1980s and '90s, exercise-and-diet culture exploded
as women began to pursue a toned, athletic body type.
Women like Jane Fonda (neon-pink leotards, anyone?) became famous for their popular exercise videos, which featured slender, toned women.

This era was followed by the supermodel era of the early
2000s, in which the emphasis went back to bone-thin body
types. Supermodels exploded in popularity and portrayed
the new ideal body, which required a close-to-starvation
diet to achieve. This body type lacked all fat and had the

appearance of an adolescent boy. Eating disorders became a huge struggle again for young women everywhere.

As the twenty-first century progressed to present day, a huge push for diversity and celebrating all body types has emerged. Although there are many positive things about this, the battle for the "ideal" body type has not gone away. With the rise of social media, women are now exposed to an endless loop of "flawless women," ranging in shape and size.

> The "ideal woman" is ever changing, and we continue to obsessively *chase* after her.

As women living in today's world, each one of us is constantly reminded that we *don't* have the curves of the Kardashians or the thin body of the Victoria's Secret model or the super-toned body of the latest fitness guru. We're not striving to fit one mold; we're trying to fit *all the molds*—all the time.

The "ideal woman" is ever changing, and we continue to obsessively chase after her.

The lies continue to taunt us day in and day out. "You are ugly. You will only be beautiful and happy once you change _____." We believe it. And we do the next thing to try to make ourselves pretty enough.

The Cult of the Young Body

Grabbing my towel and sunglasses, I (Bethany) headed for the nearest lounge chair by the pool. It was early summer in Texas, and I was on a girls' weekend with Kristen celebrating our friend's birthday at a resort. My legs were pasty white from a lack of sun exposure over the winter months, and I was ready for a tan. I removed the towel from my waist and plopped down on my chair. My pale-white legs seemed to shine in the sun. Feeling self-conscious, I glanced around to see if anyone else noticed the rays of sunshine reflecting off my legs. My fair skin was not friends with the sun, and I had always struggled to get a tan. I would see pictures of perfectly tan women and wish I could achieve that golden glow.

Determined to make today my day, I put my sunglasses on and lay back. No sunscreen this time. Just my legs and the sun. Ahhh, this was going to be fabulous.

A gentle breeze blew. *It doesn't get much better than this*, I thought. The minutes slowly turned into hours as I occasionally rotated back and forth.

As the late-afternoon sun shined above, Kristen suggested that we head in for some food. Glancing down at my legs, I was pleasantly surprised. They actually looked tan. I couldn't believe it!

As the three of us walked inside, out of the sun, the soft light of the resort lobby revealed a different story. My legs weren't tan . . . they were red. Bright red. Gently touching my skin, I realized that my legs were extremely burned. I tried to play it off by making jokes about how my pale skin refuses to tan, but inside I was kicking myself for being so stupid.

I was about to pay a big price for my vanity.

Over the next few days, the sunburn on my legs turned into dozens of blisters. I had to get special burn cream to help with the pain and healing.

My desire for a beautiful sun-kissed tan drove me to a place where I was willing to do whatever it took to get it. My body paid the price.

The blisters eventually did go away, but my legs had permanent burn damage that has lasted to this day. I had to learn the lesson the hard way. From that day on, I decided to make peace with the fact that I would never be the woman with golden beauty. Forcing my body to fit into a certain mold wasn't worth the cost.

Altering our bodies to achieve a certain look is something so common today that most of us don't even think about it. The multi-billion-dollar beauty industry reminds us regularly of how quickly we can cover that blemish, remove that mole, tan that skin, or smooth those unwanted wrinkles. From plastic surgery to injections to anti-aging creams, we are willing to go to great lengths to keep our bodies looking young and beautiful.

We are obsessed with beauty because we are told that flawless women are *better*. Young women are prettier. Wrinkle-free skin is more attractive. Cellulite and stretch marks are detestable.

> Our society has made a *cult* out of the *young body*.

Our society has made a cult out of the *young body*.

Most people don't say this out loud, but the cultural message is clear: Aging is ugly. Do whatever you can to fight against it.

Our society's obsession with idolizing the young body hasn't caused us to value our bodies more but to *hate* them. Especially as we birth children and grow older. That is why most women look in the mirror and secretly hate what they see.

In her book *Love Thy Body*, Nancy Pearcey says,

Is it true that Western culture devalues the body? Don't many people place a ridiculously high value on physical appearance and fitness? Consider the widespread obsession with diets, exercise, bodybuilding, cosmetics, plastic surgery, botox, anti-aging treatments, and so on. A Christian college professor once told me, "It seems to me that people tend to go in the opposite direction—they make an idol out of the body." But to be obsessed by the body does not mean we accept it. "The cult of the young body, the veneration of the air-brushed, media produced body, conceals our hatred for real bodies," writes theologian Beth Felker Jones of Wheaton College. "Cultural practice expresses aversion to the body."[3]

As a Christian woman, you've probably heard messages about the dangers of idolizing beauty and being careful not to overemphasize your outward appearance. But as Nancy Pearcey just pointed out, that's not your deepest problem. When you stand in front of the mirror and critique your physical body, you are revealing your deep yet subtle hatred for it. Whether you realize it or not, you are accepting the lies of the cult. You are viewing your real body as little more than a burdensome shell to be altered and changed.

Pearcey continues, "An obsession with exercising, bodybuilding, and dieting can reveal a mindset akin to that of a luxury car owner polishing and tuning up an expensive automobile. Philosophers call that 'instrumentalizing' the body, which means treating it as a tool to be used and controlled instead of valuing it for its own sake. When we do that, we objectify the body as part of nature to be conquered."[4]

The taunting lie that plays on a loop in your head is rooted in a hatred for your *real body*. When you hear the words "You are ugly. You will only be beautiful and happy once you change _____," you are hearing a godless ideology that sacrifices real women at the altar of youthfulness. When you affirm this lie in your head, you are accepting an antibiblical narrative about your body, aging, and your God-given female design.

This way of thinking does not come from Scripture and is not rooted in truth.

As Christian women, we will never get out of this beauty spiral until we reject the false narrative of culture and start thinking like a *Christian* about beauty.

Thinking Like a Christian about Beauty

You can only imagine the opportunities for comparison, jealousy, and inner beauty battles we had growing up in a home with five sisters. While hanging out in public, one sister would get a compliment on her "amazing hair" while the rest of us would sit there feeling like we had mops on our heads. Another time, a different sister would get compliments on her "gorgeous eyes" while the rest of us would wonder what was wrong with ours. This sort of thing happened all the time (and still does to this day).

Over the years, we each wrestled with our own beauty struggles and body lies. We fell prey to the worldly belief that our *real* bodies were something ugly that needed to be altered and changed. We were not thinking about our bodies or beauty like *Christians*. We were thinking about them like the world. And this only fueled our discontentment and struggle.

As the two of us (Kristen and Bethany) grew older, we began to realize how unbiblical our view of beauty actually was. As the two oldest sisters in the family, we were determined to grow in this area so that we could lead our younger sisters down a better path. As we began studying God's Word and asking Him to help us see His vision for feminine beauty, our mindsets began to radically change.

We started to think *like a Christian* about beauty. And that transformed everything. Here are the four biggest truths that changed our perspective:

1. Your Real Body Is a Gift

Your physical body was given to you by your Creator as a gift. Legs, hips, hair, birthmarks, and all. It's a blessing. Your womanly frame and feminine physique were made in the likeness of God's very image (see Gen. 2). Your body is not an ugly burden or a tool to be shaped but rather a physical reminder of the God who made you.

Instead of ungratefully critiquing yourself in the mirror, change your attitude to one of gratitude. When you look in the mirror, thank God for the gift of your *real* body and the blessing of your physical capabilities. Praise God for the way He created you to reflect His image. Turn your whining into worship by joining the psalmist in saying, "I praise you [God], for I am fearfully and wonderfully made. Wonderful are your works; my soul knows it very well" (Ps. 139:14).

2. Fear the Lord, Not the Mirror

The cosmetic industry has no fear of God. It bombards you with shiny new tricks to stay young, fueling the cult of youthfulness in your heart. But here's the truth. It doesn't matter how perfect a woman's face is today, give it fifty years and it will not look the same. Physical beauty cannot last forever. That's why Proverbs 31 calls our attention to what truly matters. "Charm is deceitful, and beauty is vain, but a woman who fears the LORD is to be praised" (v. 30). Fearing the Lord means you care more about pleasing God with your life than pleasing people. When you fear the Lord above all else, you will no longer be a slave to the opinions of the makeup industry or social media because you won't be living for their approval. You will be free to live for the glory and honor of your King.

3. Your Heart Matters More Than Your Hair

The real enemy of your soul (Satan) would love nothing more than to deceive you into valuing the temporal over the *eternal*. He knows that what you treasure will capture your heart. That's why it's so important to remember that what matters most in God's economy isn't the condition of your hair but the condition of your heart. As a redeemed daughter of God, you were given your body by your Creator *so that* you could serve Him with it. You are more than a pretty decoration to look at. Your body has God-given purpose that may include the ability to work, hands to help, a womb to bear children, vocal cords to sing, and so on, for the good of others and the glory of God. Your existence is an embodied one for these greater purposes. First Corinthians 6:19–20 says, "Do you not know that your body is a temple of the Holy Spirit within you, whom you have from God? You are not your own, for you were bought with a price. So glorify God in your body." Beauty will come and go, but the way we serve God and glorify Him will last for eternity.

4. Physical Brokenness Won't Last Forever

We live in a fallen world that has been deeply impacted by sin. Everything in our lives, including our bodies, has felt this impact. As a result, we will suffer physical things that are not considered "ideal" (like sickness, chronic pain, deformities, skin conditions, etc.). But even as we view these challenges from a godly perspective and seek contentment toward God for His providence in how He created us, we don't have to pretend that everything is just right. We can acknowledge the brokenness we experience while at the same time reminding our hearts of the eternal hope we have in Christ. Philippians 3:20–21 says that "our citizenship is in heaven, and from it we await a Savior, the Lord Jesus Christ, who will transform our lowly body to be like his glorious body, by the power that enables him even to subject all things to himself." One day, He will make things *just right* according to His perfect perspective and original design for us as His image bearers.

For a Christian woman, learning to view your body through a biblical lens is the key to combating beauty lies. You will never change the way you feel about your body until you change the way you think about your body.

You have to begin viewing your body, beauty, and purpose like a *Christian*.

As one author from Got Questions warns, "We must watch out for anything that draws us away from God, including the too-often extreme emphasis the world places on appearances. . . . We should be humble, not committing idolatry in worshiping the creation rather than the Creator (Col. 3:5)."[5]

However, this doesn't mean we shouldn't care about our outward appearance. There is a balance. God created women to be feminine and lovely, and it's good to embrace that. Engaging in routines like brushing our hair, wearing makeup, painting our nails, and taking care of our bodies (through exercise and nutrition) can be lovely expressions of our femininity. Each of these areas is a matter of the heart and of personal conviction. We (Kristen and Bethany) believe these things can be embraced and enjoyed in a way that honors God if our hearts are in the right place.

> God created women to be *feminine* and lovely, and it's good to embrace that.

As one writer points out, "A woman's . . . outward appearance is not the measure of her beauty or worth. Being made in the image of God is that measure, and it makes all of us equally valuable, from fertilization to death, regardless of age, ability, or appearance."[6]

The glitz and glam may be alluring, but they will fade as fast as they come. When the lies taunt you by saying, "You are ugly. You will only be beautiful and happy once you change _____," you can fearlessly respond by saying, "My body is fearfully and wonderfully made. My worth comes from God, and my purpose is to worship Him. I am no longer a slave to this world but am living for the glory of my King."

Chapter 11 Study Guide

"Your body is not an ugly burden or a tool to be shaped but rather a physical reminder of the God who made you. When you look in the mirror, thank God for the gift of your real body and the blessing of your physical capabilities."

1. How old were you when you first started thinking about physical beauty?

_____

_____

2. When you look in the mirror, which parts of your body do you currently struggle to embrace with gratitude? Check all that apply.

☐ Face ☐ Hair ☐ Hands

☐ Nose ☐ Breasts ☐ Legs

☐ Lips ☐ Stomach ☐ Butt

☐ Eyes ☐ Arms ☐ Feet

☐ Other _____

What is fueling your dissatisfaction with those areas of your body?

_____

_____

_____

3. In what ways do you need to begin thinking about your body and beauty more like a *Christian* woman?

_____

_____

_____

4. Proverbs 31:30 reminds us that "charm is deceitful, and beauty is vain, but a woman who fears the LORD is to be praised." How would your perspective on beauty change if you feared the Lord more than the mirror?

_____

_____

_____

5. Take a few minutes to practice gratitude for the body God gave you. Think of five specific things you can thank Him for right now:

   a. _____

   b. _____

   c. _____

   d. _____

   e. _____

6. Finish this prayer in your own words: *Dear Lord, I praise You because my body is fearfully and wonderfully made. I know that my worth comes from You and my purpose is to worship You. I no*

longer want to be a slave to this world, but I desire to live for Your glory alone. Help me to . . .

_____

_____

_____

_____

_____

_____

Part 4

RECLAIMING GOD'S TIMELESS DESIGN

chapter 12

I'm a W.O.M.A.N.

The two of us stood in the meet-and-greet line with nerves through the ceiling. We might have looked calm on the outside, but we were shaking in our boots on the inside.

This was our moment. Our chance to meet one of our personal heroes of the faith. Nancy DeMoss Wolgemuth (Nancy Leigh DeMoss at that time). She is a Christian celebrity of sorts . . . at least to the two of us. We had both been deeply impacted by her books as young women and credit much of our growth in biblical womanhood to Nancy's faithfulness and ministry.

The year was 2010 (four years before we founded Girl Defined Ministries), and the two of us were passionate about living out our Christian faith. We wanted to reach younger women with the truth of God's design for their lives, but we didn't know exactly how to do that.

The two of us decided that writing a book could be an amazing way to reach younger women. We had a problem, though. We had zero connections. Zero contacts. Zero platform. Zero ministry. And zero clue on how to actually get a book out into the world.

So we did what any inexperienced hopeful authors do. We wrote a manuscript. Yep, long before we ever became published authors, we wrote a manuscript and called it *Models Wanted*. This book was all about calling women to be models for Jesus. We took this idea even further and decided we needed to get it into the hands of someone who could make something of it.

We literally printed out the entire manuscript, along with a personal letter to Nancy Leigh DeMoss, and took it with us to her ministry's annual conference called the True Woman Conference.

And that brings us back to the meet-and-greet line. We wanted to give Nancy a copy of *Models Wanted* and ask her to endorse it. A big, bold ask on our part. Nancy had no idea who the two of us were, and she had hundreds of people waiting in line to greet her. I guess we figured if we didn't shoot for the stars, we wouldn't hit them.

The moment came and we finally got to meet Nancy. She was just as kind and godly as we'd imagined. She graciously took our huge stack of papers and let us know she'd have someone reach out to us when they'd taken a look. We walked away from that line feeling excited over the possibility of Nancy having a copy of our book.

Nancy kept her word, and a team member from her ministry contacted us about the book. They let us know that Nancy didn't have the capacity to read through and endorse

Models Wanted but that we were invited to start blogging for them on the branch of their ministry geared toward teenage girls. A huge opportunity for two nobodies from Texas. We were thrilled and counted it a big win.

Fast-forward to 2014.

The *Models Wanted* book never got published, but the idea eventually morphed into what is now Girl Defined Ministries. We launched our little *Girl Defined* blog and started posting faithfully three days a week. Let's just say that God can use even the smallest of efforts. Within months of writing in our humble little corner of the internet, we received an email from an acquisitions editor at Baker Books asking us if we'd like to sign a contract to become authors.

This had to be spam.

We were two nobodies from Texas.

There was *no way* we were getting asked to become published authors by one of the largest Christian publishing houses in America.

That's exactly what was happening, though.

Little did we know that God had a big plan for these two bloggers from Texas. Not only did we sign a contract to write our first book, *Girl Defined: God's Radical Design for Beauty, Femininity, and Identity*, but we also later received an endorsement from Nancy Leigh DeMoss for that book. Talk about a full-circle moment.

> He is looking for women who desire to be *faithful* with exactly what He's given them.

This entire experience taught the two of us a big lesson about God. He isn't looking for the most famous or well-known women to make an impact for His kingdom. He is looking for women who desire to be faithful with exactly what He's given them. Women who, like Mary the mother of Jesus, say, "Behold, I am the servant of the Lord; let it be to me according to your word" (Luke 1:38). Women who desire to live fearless lives for the applause of their King and not the applause of this world.

The two of us weren't perfect in this area, but we had a desire to live for our King. We wanted to live for Jesus. We wanted to serve Him. We wanted to reach others with the truths of God's Word. We wanted to live boldly for Him. Somehow, someway, and for reasons we will never understand, God blessed our meager efforts. This book is in your hands because of His kindness in our lives. We're committed to pointing women back to Jesus as long as He has us alive and breathing.

God doesn't need you to be someone famous, wealthy, or with supermodel looks to be used by Him. He just wants you to be a woman who says, "I am a servant of the Lord. Help me to do your will." A woman who says, "I am a gospel-redeemed woman, and I want to live in line with my truest identity in Christ." It's actually a very simple call. It's a heart that is focused on serving and glorifying Him.

I'm a W.O.M.A.N.

God is looking for women who are willing to follow Him. Women who are willing to worship Him above all else. Women who know they're weak and in need of His strength. To be among the few who are willing to reject the lies of feminism and embrace gospel-redeemed womanhood instead. Will you be one of those women?

We created an acrostic of the word WOMAN to help you in this pursuit. We know living out fearless femininity can be a challenge. Here's a simple tool to remind you of your identity as a woman of God.

W = Worth Is Found in Christ

Your worth is not found in your looks, accomplishments, accolades, or anything else you can be or do. Your worth is found in the blood of Jesus and what He did for you on the cross. You never have to be good enough, because He was already good enough for you. Whenever you're feeling overwhelmed or down, remember that Christ has adopted you into His family as His daughter. You have a new identity as a redeemed daughter of God. Remind yourself that you are His. Your worth is found in His great love for you.

O = Order with Her Gender

Remind yourself regularly that God designed men and women to be equally valuable but purposely different. This is a truth about gender that needs to be said over and over again. God designed gender to have order. Men and women are not the same, and that's okay. It's time to champion those differences and say, "God knew what He was doing when He created men and women, and it's a good thing." His order for gender, family, and the church is for our flourishing and His glory.

M = Meek in Spirit

Yes, the Bible actually calls women to be meek and gentle in spirit (see 1 Pet. 3:3–4). It's a heart posture of humility.

Think back to the type of woman Margaret Sanger was encouraging women to be. It was the opposite of meek. She wanted women to be loud and brash like she was in the early days of her misguided feminism. God wants the opposite for His daughters. One of our author friends, Rebekah Hargraves, describes it this way:

> The Greek word translated "meek" is "praus," and it literally means "mildness of disposition, gentleness of spirit." . . . Having a meek and quiet spirit has much more to do with what is going on in your heart than it does the outward picture you are presenting. . . . What having a "meek and quiet spirit" actually means is that you go through life largely at peace. You do not fear the future, because you know your God.[1]

This is the heart posture of a godly woman.

A = Anchored in Truth

When your heart is anchored in truth, you won't be swept up by the enticing messages around you. Just like a boat anchors to a secure source, you can anchor to your secure God. He is the same yesterday, today, and forever. His Word is timeless. Rather than trying to measure up to the ever-changing standards of our society (just like we saw in chapter 11), choose to live according to timeless truths. The woman who anchors her heart in truth is free to live out fearless femininity. She understands that her strength is found in a God bigger than herself. That brings freedom.

N = Noble in Character

Noble character. That's how the famous Proverbs 31:10 starts out: "A wife of noble character who can find? She is worth far more than rubies" (NIV). The character of the woman is what's most important throughout the rest of that passage. Jessica Brodie, an award-winning novelist and journalist, describes it this way: "A woman of noble character is honest, hardworking, trustworthy, and wise, like Ruth. She is loyal and dependable, striving to serve the Lord and do what is right rather than gain power, success, or wealth. She is also kind and compassionate, and generous to others."[2] Many women have climbed the corporate ladder, won the medals, or achieved worldly success only to find it wasn't enough. That's because God created us to ultimately find complete worth in Him. A woman does not need worldly accolades to experience deep satisfaction. Focus on becoming the kind of woman God says is praiseworthy.

Living Out Faithful Womanhood

Tragedy and heartache were no strangers to Ruth. She lost her husband after ten years of marriage. To make her heartbreak even worse, she lost her brother-in-law and her father-in-law as well.

These deaths were life shattering for Ruth.

She lived during a time when women were all but destitute without a husband to provide for and protect them. She had no rights. No land. No future. What was she to do?

She had a choice to make. Go home to her people of Moab and try to find a new husband or follow her also widowed mother-in-law to a faraway land. A land foreign to Ruth. A people foreign to Ruth.

Although Ruth was grieving the loss of her husband and dealing with her own unknown future, she had compassion in her heart. She loved her mother-in-law, Naomi, and she loved the God of Israel she'd come to know because of marrying into this family. Ruth chose to follow Naomi and care for her as a blood daughter would. In the book of Ruth, we read that famous verse where she tells Naomi, "For where you go I will go, and where you lodge I will lodge. Your people shall be my people, and your God my God" (Ruth 1:16).

Ruth was laying down her life and future to care for her aging mother-in-law. She didn't have to do this. She could have easily chosen the surer path. No one would have blamed her for returning to her people in Moab and trying to secure a future for herself. Ruth was a woman of deep character, though. A woman who had a genuine love for God and wanted to be with His people. She wanted to continue to know Him. Her faith in God was strong, and she trusted Him to provide for her future.

The Lord blessed Ruth's faith and provided in a way she never could have anticipated. The pastors and theologians over at GotQuestions.org bring great insight into Ruth's situation:

Ruth trusted the Lord, and He rewarded her faithfulness by giving her not only a husband but a son (Obed), a grandson (Jesse), and a great-grandson named David, the king of Israel (Ruth 4:17). Besides these gifts (Psalm 127:3), God gave Ruth the blessing of being listed in the lineage of Jesus (Matthew 1:5).

Ruth is an example of how God can change a life and take it in a direction He has foreordained. We see Him working out His perfect plan in Ruth's life, just as He does with all His children (Romans 8:28). Although Ruth came from a pagan background in Moab, once she met the God of Israel, she became a living testimonial to Him by faith. Even though she lived in humble circumstances before marrying Boaz, she believed that God was faithful to care for His people.[3]

One woman. Willing to trust God. Willing to follow Him wherever He would lead. Her faithfulness was blessed, and she was included in the most important family tree ever to exist. This is a woman who lived out her identity as a daughter of God in a bold and courageous way. She didn't allow her external circumstances to determine her future. She trusted in the one who designed her and lived fully for His glory. And the Lord blessed her faithfulness.

Faithful women are needed like never before. Will you rise to the calling? Pursuing God's design for your womanhood takes a reliance on Him. It takes knowing His Word. Let's be women who are focused on living for our King. With God's help, we can be women of faith. *All for His glory.*

Chapter 12 Study Guide

"God is looking for women who are willing to follow Him. Women who are willing to worship Him above all else. Women who know they're weak and in need of His strength. To be among the few who are willing to reject the lies of feminism and embrace gospel-redeemed womanhood instead."

1. Describe what it looks like to be a faithful Christian woman.

_____

_____

2. Fill in the acrostic for the word WOMAN.

W =

O =

M =

A =

N =

3. How does the following quote change your view of yourself?

   "Your worth is not found in your looks, accomplishments, ac-colades, or anything else you can be or do. Your worth is found in the blood of Jesus and what He did for you on the cross."

   _____

   _____

   _____

4. How did Ruth's faithfulness impact her future?

   _____

   _____

5. Write out a simple prayer asking God to grow your faith and help you live a life fully focused on Him.

   _____

   _____

   _____

   _____

chapter 13

Living Out Fearless Femininity

I t's a bold thing to ask—but I think it will work," our friend said, looking at the two of us. We (Kristen and Bethany) were meeting up with a friend to discuss *Cosmopolitan* magazine (of all things). Our local grocery store chain had been carrying the magazine for decades, and we were tired of getting bombarded by its lewd covers every time we grabbed a loaf of bread.

"Not to mention the magazine is placed at eye level for any child passing by to see. That's not okay," Bethany said with a hint of frustration in her voice.

We nodded in agreement.

"So, what's our plan?" I (Kristen) asked with excitement.

"Okay," our friend started, "first, we recruit as many women as possible who feel the same way we do about the magazine. Next, we encourage everyone to call the operation manager at the store headquarters. Here's his direct line. We make the same request: 'Remove *Cosmo* from your shelves.'"

The plan was bold. Gutsy. Ambitious. We liked it.

"Let's do it," Bethany said, standing up with a determined smile.

Over the next week, we rallied dozens of other women from our community toward this cause. They all felt the same way we did and were eager to jump on board. Without warning, the chief operations manager of this popular grocery store chain was suddenly inundated by women asking for the same thing.

Get rid of Cosmo.

"I'm tired of having to see *Cosmo*'s raunchy and explicit magazine cover every time I check out at your store," I said to the manager on the phone. "It's degrading to women and inappropriate for children."

"I understand, ma'am," he said. "But I'm not sure I can do anything about it."

I wasn't giving up that easily.

"You claim to be a family-friendly grocery store, yet you place this trashy magazine in every checkout aisle in every single one of your stores."

"I get it, ma'am. Truly I do. And I actually agree with you. But again—I'm not sure what I can do."

"Just promise me you'll do something? Talk to someone higher up about this?"

"I will, ma'am. I can definitely do that."

"Thank you." And with that, I hung up the phone.

Nothing happened right away, but over the next few months, some changes actually began to take place.

Our little cohort of women texted back and forth with one another about what we saw. The grocery store chain had added "blockers" to all of their *Cosmo* magazines. These are little plastic strips that sit in front of the magazine cover, blocking the provocative wording.

This was a good start, but not good enough.

Continuing our campaign, we were determined to have full victory. After all, we were women. We were the target audience for this magazine. *And we didn't want it.*

We pressed on.

To our shock and amazement, the grocery store chain actually began listening to us. Our small group of passionate ladies brought about massive change.

As the year came to a close, we noticed something extraordinary happen. We no longer saw *Cosmo* featured on any of their shelves.

It had been completely removed.

The *Cosmo* Girl was gone.

We were excited and amazed that our efforts had worked. Our voice had been heard.

A Long Line of Fearless Femininity

It was an eye-opening experience for the two of us to see what a small group of determined women could accomplish. By putting our efforts together to stand for what we believed in, we were able to make huge changes.

We don't want *Cosmopolitan* magazine in our faces anymore. We're done accepting the shallow and degrading lifestyle pushed on us by the *Cosmo* Girl. We're calling out the propaganda for what it is. We're done accepting the feminist lies. We're chasing something *much better.*

As Christian women, we don't have to be afraid of this world or its lies because we're not here for them. We're here for our King. We can fearlessly stand on the rock-solid truth of God's design for our womanhood because our strength comes from Him. Our dependence on Him empowers us to live as faithful daughters for His glory. Our mission isn't to build our own perfect little lives . . . but to further His gospel message. To spread His Word. To share His truth. To fight back against lies. To expose the darkness.

He is what drives us forward without fear.

As Christian women, each one of us comes from a long line of courageous and fearless women. Throughout the Bible we see numerous examples of these inspiring ladies. They are our heroes of the faith. We are a part of their legacy. Just like we are today, these women were on a mission for God in their time. They stood against the cultural trends of their day and showed incredible faith and trust in the Lord. They were fearless because their identity and purpose were anchored in the Lord. They knew *Whose* they were. And they did incredible things as a result.

Rahab

Born into a pagan land and living as a prostitute, Rahab had no personal teaching about God. She had heard stories of Him, though. *Miraculous* stories. And this filled her with fear and awe. In her heart, she believed that the God of Israel was the one true God. Putting her life on the line, she chose to protect the Israelite men who came to spy out her land. When they came to her house, she boldly declared, "The Lord your God, he is God in the heavens above and on the earth beneath" (Josh. 2:11). She knew *who* God was. And she risked everything to follow Him. God gave Rahab faith to fear Him and to defy the order of the King of Jericho (see Josh. 2:1–21).

Esther

Born as a Jew but living as an exile in a foreign land, Esther had a life that was anything but easy. Having lost both of her parents, she was being raised by her cousin when her life changed forever. Her physical beauty caught the eye of the king, and she was taken to his palace, where she eventually became his new queen. When facts surrounding the slaughter of her people (the Jews) became known to her, she secretly called for three days of fasting among her people. Then she said, "I will go to the king, though it is against the law, and if I perish, I perish" (Esther 4:16). Putting her life on the line in faith, Esther acted courageously to save God's people. She trusted God with the outcome of her life, and God used her to save thousands of Jews as a result. He gave her faith to risk her life for the sake of her people.

Mary

Growing up in the land of Israel, Mary probably had a fairly ordinary life, living with her family and helping them make ends meet. Then, out of nowhere, an angel from God appeared to her to say that *she* was God's chosen woman to give birth to the Messiah. The news that she would conceive this baby as a *virgin* probably sent shock waves down her spine. The Jewish culture she lived in did not look kindly upon pregnancies out of wedlock. But rather than responding in terror and fear, Mary anchored her heart in the Lord and trusted Him. She humbly said, "Behold, I am the servant of the Lord; let it be to me according to your word" (Luke 1:38). God gave Mary faith to trust Him and to act fearlessly.

These women did not have easy lives. They faced many challenges and hardships. But they, along with countless others (Sarah, Hannah, Ruth, Abigail, Elizabeth, and Lydia, to name a few more), were fearless because of their trust and hope in the Lord. Their identity was rooted in Him. This is our lineage. This is our heritage. We come from a long line of *fearless femininity*.

When a woman puts her trust in the Lord and follows Him with her whole heart, she is freed to obey Him and trust that His plans for her life are good and that He will accomplish His will. She lives without fear because she knows that God is good and does good (see Ps. 119:68). Even when life is challenging, painful, or filled with grief, she clings to the truth that He will work all things for the good of those who love Him and are called according to His purposes (see Rom. 8:28). When she feels tired and weak, she calls to mind verses like Galatians 6:9, which says, "Let us not grow weary of doing good, for in due season we will reap, if we do not give up."

In the good and the hard, her life becomes a vessel that God uses for His purposes and glory.

Sisters on Mission Together

Landing in Poland for the first time, we (Kristen and Bethany) were excited to be speaking at a local women's conference in Warsaw. We had connected with the leader of their women's ministry through social media the year prior and had developed a long-distance friendship. Rounding the corner at the airport, we were greeted by a whole group of excited Polish women holding a large sign in English that said, "Welcome, Kristen and Bethany!"

Over the next week, we grew to love those women. We spent time in their homes and got to know their culture, their food, and even some of their language. Despite the fact that we lived thousands of miles apart, in completely different countries, we had the most important thing in common: *We loved Jesus.* These women were passionate about God's design for biblical femininity and were eager to hear us share about it at the conference. They were hungry for the Word and excited to learn about God's design for womanhood.

We left that trip feeling grateful and inspired. Seeing those Polish women on fire for God reminded us that we are a part of a *global sisterhood.* Those women are our sisters in Christ and are on the same mission as us—to *glorify God.*

Regardless of where a woman is born or what type of background she comes from, in Christ we are all the same. We are all redeemed daughters of God, saved by the grace of Jesus. Our identity, purpose, and mission are the *same.* We are each called to live for God's glory and to be on mission for Him. The Great Commission that Jesus gave to His disciples is our mission as well. "Go therefore and make disciples of all nations . . . teaching them to observe all that

I have commanded you. And behold, I am with you always, to the end of the age" (Matt. 28:19–20).

God is calling you to live out this mission right now, right where He has you. Whether you're single or married, have kids or don't, your job is to make disciples by teaching others the truth about Jesus. Your calling is to follow God and His ways.

When you follow God's Word over the world's ways, you make the gospel *believable* to those watching you. When you choose to reject the lies of feminist womanhood, you point others toward God's better plan for femininity. When you fight against the ditch of religious womanhood, you

> Regardless of where a woman is *born* or what type of background she comes from, in Christ we are all the *same*.

show others the need for dependence on God and His grace. When you push back against the sexualization of womanhood today, you reveal that women were given immense worth and dignity by their Creator. When you honor the marriage bed by embracing sex rightly, you honor the covenant and point others back to the covenant-keeping God. When you fight against the lies of beauty culture and the cosmetic industry, you become living proof that a woman's identity and happiness can come only from God. When you cherish your kids, prioritize your family, and love your husband well, you display a compelling picture of a gospel-shaped family.

When you live every part of your womanhood in surrender to God, your life becomes a beautiful act of worship back to Him.

Made to Be She

Over sixty years ago, a troubled young woman named Kate Millett set out to destroy biblical womanhood. Her mission was to obliterate society's acceptance of God's design for traditional marriage, gender roles, morality, and the family. She gathered women together in "consciousness-raising" groups, and they recited chants back and forth, affirming their mission.

Sadly, Kate's mission was highly successful. The influence of one woman's toxic ideas would eventually impact the lives of millions of women worldwide.

It's time for us to reclaim what has been lost.

It's time to stand up for what has been torn down. It's time for us to use our influence to rebuild what has been broken. If one woman with passion and zeal could influence so many women to embrace lies, think about what we could do to influence women to embrace truth. As Mary Kassian once boldly stated, "I'm praying that God is going to raise up a counterrevolution of women. Women who hold the knowledge of our times in one hand and the truth, clarity, and charity of the Word of God in the other."[1]

It's time for us, as Christian women, to reclaim God's good design for fearless femininity.

We have been silent for far too long. It's time to stand up for what is right and true. For what is good and beautiful. Just as Kate Millett found strength in numbers, we can do the same. God has given us the body of Christ so that we don't have to live this life alone. Let's link arms with the Christian sisterhood and lean into that support. Deepening our relationships with one another through our local gospel-centered churches will strengthen us for this mission.

We won't be gathering together to "raise our conscious-ness," but we should be gathering together for prayer, en-couragement, the studying of the Word, and fellowship. Just as Millett called out her vision of womanhood through catchy chants and cheers, we need to regularly vocalize and affirm our biblical mission to one another.

Why do women exist?
To glorify God!
What is our mission?
To be kingdom-minded women!
Who designed us?
God!
Who defines us?
Our Maker!
How do we honor God with our lives?
By worshiping Him above all else!
How do we change the world around us?
By fighting the lies of this world and fearlessly pursuing God's truth!
How do we do this?
By seeking God and depending on Him for strength and wisdom!
Why does womanhood matter?
Because our femininity was created to point others back to the God who made us!

We are women. *Made to be she.* Everything about our body, beauty, gender, femininity, reproduction, identity, and purpose has been given to us by our Creator. He is our Maker. The One who designed us gets to define us. We will only find our true purpose and identity when we stop chasing the ways of this world and start chasing the ways of our Lord. We are His. Created on purpose and for a purpose. Our femininity was given to us so that we would bring glory and honor to our King.

It's time to reclaim God's plan for fearless femininity.

Chapter 13 Study Guide

"When a woman puts her trust in the Lord and follows Him with her whole heart, she is freed to obey Him and trust that His plans for her life are good and that He will accomplish His will."

1. Think of one woman you know who has faithfully followed God and lived out fearless femininity in her life. How does her life encourage you?

_____

_____

2. What are the top three areas in which you need God's help to live more fearlessly and faithfully for Him?

   a. _____

   b. _____

   c. _____

3. How has this book impacted your view of womanhood? What is the most powerful thing you learned?

_____

_____

_____

4. In this chapter, we looked at Matthew 28:19–20. How can you obey God's call to make disciples right where He has you?

_____

_____

5. If you benefited from the wisdom of this book, don't keep it to yourself! Can you think of one friend who needs to hear the message of God's design for womanhood? If so, we challenge you to do one of the following:

- Give her your copy of this book and encourage her to read it.
- Buy her this book as a gift and tell her it's a must-read.
- Invite her to read this book alongside you and discuss the book together.
- Invite a small group of women to do a book study together.

ACKNOWLEDGMENTS

God . . . thank You first and foremost for giving us the opportunity to write another book and for the much-needed strength in this busy season of motherhood.

Zack and David . . . our lifelong supporters. Thank you for being there for us for book number six!

Candice Watters, Bethel Grove, Molly Maller, and Crossway Bible Church elders . . . we can't thank you enough for your wisdom and feedback on the first draft. This book is stronger because of you.

Rebekah Von Lintel . . . thank you for believing in us over the past ten years.

Baker Books . . . your team is incredible. We have truly loved working with every single person at Baker. Thank you for partnering with us to publish *Made to Be She*.

Friends who supported us along the way . . . thanks for sticking with us through yet another book. We're grateful for you!

Girl Defined sisterhood . . . your constant love, support, and encouragement never cease to amaze us. You have been with us every step of the way, and we love you!

NOTES

Chapter 1 Seduced by the *Cosmo* Girl

1. Leanne Bayley, "Caitlyn Jenner Won Big at GLAMOUR's Woman of the Year Awards," *Glamour*, November 10, 2015, https://www.glamourmagazine.co.uk/article/caitlyn-jenner-glamour-women-of-the-year-awards-america.

2. Russell Falcon, "Dallas Drag Queen Event for Kids Sparks Outrage, Defense," The Hill, June 7, 2022, https://thehill.com/homenews/wire/3514357-dallas-drag-queen-event-for-kids-sparks-outrage-defense/.

3. Heather Heying, "The Torment and Tragedy of Teenage Girls," Natural Selections, June 14, 2022, https://naturalselections.substack.com/p/the-torment-and-tragedy-of-teenage.

4. *Obergefell v. Hodges (2015)*, National Constitution Center, accessed November 20, 2023, https://constitutioncenter.org/the-constitution/supreme-court-case-library/obergefell-v-hodges.

5. "Feminism," *History*, accessed on December 20, 2023, https://www.history.com/topics/womens-history/feminism-womens-history.

6. Betty Friedan, *The Feminine Mystique* (repr. New York: Dell/Laurel, 1984), 144.

7. Quoted in Lynn Sherr, "What Has Been Done and Should Be Done," *New York Times*, October 5, 1975, https://www.nytimes.com/1975/10/05/archives/what-has-been-done-and-should-be-done-the-politics-of-womens.html.

8. Quoted in Paul Senz, "Former *Cosmo* Writer: 'I Wrote This Book as an Act of Atonement,'" *Catholic World Report*, July 28, 2020, https://www.catholicworldreport.com/2020/07/28/former-cosmo-writer-i-wrote-this-book-as-an-act-of-atonement/.

9. Sue Ellen Browder, *Subverted: How I Helped the Sexual Revolution Hijack the Women's Movement* (San Francisco: Ignatius Press, 2015), 37–39.

10. Robert Reinhold, "Census Finds Unmarried Couples Have Doubled from 1970 to 1978," *New York Times*, June 27, 1979, https://www.nytimes.com/1979/06/27/archives/census-finds-unmarried-couples-have-doubled-from-1970-to-1978.html.

11. Browder, *Subverted*, 37.

12. Debra J. Brody and Qiuping Gu, "Antidepressant Use among Adults: United States, 2015–2018," Centers for Disease Control and Prevention, September 2020, https://www.cdc.gov/nchs/products/databriefs/db377.htm.

13. Carrie Gress, "Why Don't We Tell Women What's Making Them Miserable?," *National Review*, August 29, 2021, https://www.nationalreview.com/2021/08/why-dont-we-tell-women-whats-making-them-miserable/.

14. Mary Kassian, "Recognizing Feminist Thought," *Revive Our Hearts* (podcast), April 30, 2014, https://www.reviveourhearts.com/podcast/revive-our-hearts/recognizing-feminist-thought-1/.

15. Kristen Clark and Bethany Baird, *Girl Defined: God's Radical Design for Beauty, Femininity, and Identity* (Grand Rapids: Baker Books, 2016), 21.

Chapter 2 The Ditch of Feminist Womanhood

1. Sarah Pruitt, "What Are the Four Waves of Feminism?," *History*, accessed November 27, 2023, https://www.history.com/news/feminism-four-waves.

2. Sharon James, *God's Design for Women in an Age of Gender Confusion* (Welwyn Garden City, UK: Evangelical Press, 2019), 40.

3. James, *God's Design for Women*, 40–41.

4. James, *God's Design for Women*, 41.

5. Carolyn McCulley, *Radical Womanhood: Feminine Faith in a Feminist World* (Chicago: Moody, 2008), 46.

6. Mary A. Kassian and Nancy DeMoss Wolgemuth, *True Woman 101: Divine Design: An Eight-Week Study on Biblical Womanhood* (Chicago: Moody, 2012), 131.

7. Quoted in Carl N. Degler, *At Odds: Women and the Family in America from the Revolution to the Present* (New York: Oxford University Press, 1980), 353.

8. Nancey Pearcey, *The Toxic War on Masculinity: How Christianity Reconciles the Sexes* (Grand Rapids: Baker Books, 2023), 99–100.

9. James, *God's Design for Women*, 11.

10. James, *God's Design for Women*, 37.

11. Friedan, *Feminine Mystique*, chap. 1 title.

12. Friedan, *Feminine Mystique*, 13.

13. Friedan, *Feminine Mystique*, 32.

14. Germaine Greer, *The Female Eunuch* (New York: Paladin, 1971), 319.

15. James, *God's Design for Women*, 42–43.

16. McCulley, *Radical Womanhood*, 165–66.

17. Wendy Shalit, *Girls Gone Mild: Young Women Reclaim Self-Respect and Find It's Not Bad to Be Good* (New York: Random House, 2007), 215.

18. Shalit, *Girls Gone Mild*, 210.

19. Gloria Steinem, "After Black Power, Women's Liberation," *New York Magazine*, April 4, 1969, https://nymag.com/news/politics/46802/.

20. Kyle Smith, "The Takeaway from KBJ: She Can't Define a Woman," *National Review*, March 23, 2022, https://www.nationalreview.com/corner/the-takeaway-from-kbj-she-cant-define-a-woman/.

21. Merriam-Webster Dictionary, s.v. "woman," accessed November 23, 2023, https://www.merriam-webster.com/dictionary/woman.

22. Brittney McNamara, "International Women's Day 2019: 17 Women Share What Womanhood Means to Them," *Teen Vogue*, March 8, 2019, https://www.teenvogue.com/gallery/international-womens-day-2019-what-womanhood-means.

23. Betsey Stevenson and Justin Wolfers, "The Paradox of Declining Female Happiness," pdf, University of Pennsylvania, October 16, 2008, https://law.yale.edu/sites/default/files/documents/pdf/Intellectual_Life/Stevenson_ParadoxDecliningFemaleHappiness_Dec08.pdf.

Chapter 3 The Ditch of Religious Womanhood

1. Marshall Segal, "Did We Kiss Purity Culture Goodbye?," Desiring God, March 11, 2022, https://www.desiringgod.org/articles/did-we-kiss-purity-goodbye.

2. Mimi Haddad, "A Brief History of CBE," CBE International, accessed December 21, 2023, https://www.cbeinternational.org/resource/brief-history-cbe/.

3. Mary Kassian, "Complementarianism for Dummies," The Gospel Coalition, September 4, 2012, https://www.thegospelcoalition.org/article/complementarianism-for-dummies/.

4. Chris Brooks, "What's Behind the Deconstruction Movement?," Woodside Bible Church, January 19, 2022, https://woodsidebible.org/read/whats-behind-the-deconstruction-movement/.

5. Michael Kruger, "What Is Progressive Christianity?," Reformed Theological Seminary, November 3, 2020, https://rts.edu/resources/what-is-progressive-christianity/.

Chapter 4 When Being a Royal Isn't Enough

1. Quoted in Laura Hampson, "It's Been 25 Years Since Diana Died—Why Hasn't the Treatment of Women by the Royal Family Changed?," *Independent*, August 31, 2022, https://www.independent.co.uk/life-style/royal-family/diana-death-royal-family-women-meghan-markle-b2156443.html.

2. Martin Bashir, "The Princess and the Press: Diana's 1995 BBC Interview," *Frontline*, accessed January 6, 2024, https://www.pbs.org/wgbh/pages/frontline/shows/royals/interviews/bbc.html.

3. Wikipedia, s.v. "People's Princess," accessed January 6, 2024, https://en.wikipedia.org/wiki/People%27s_princess.

4. "How Do You Find Your Identity?," Quora, accessed November 29, 2023, https://www.quora.com/How-do-you-find-your-identity.

5. Jon Bloom, "Lay Aside the Weight of Insecurity," Desiring God, January 24, 2017, https://www.desiringgod.org/articles/lay-aside-the-weight-of-insecurity.

6. Clark and Baird, *Girl Defined*, 153.

7. Jen Wilkin, "Women, Trade Self-Worth for Awe and Wonder," Desiring God, July 14, 2016, https://www.desiringgod.org/articles/women-trade-self-worth-for-awe-and-wonder.

Chapter 5 Rejecting Weak and Wimpy Womanhood

1. Trillia Newbell, "Bible Literacy for All: A Conversation with Jen Wilkin," The Gospel Coalition, November 22, 2016, https://www.thegospelcoalition.org/article/bible-literacy-for-all-conversation-with-jen-wilkin/.

2. Alyssa Poblete, "3 Reasons Women Need Good Theology," The Gospel Coalition, March 11, 2015, https://www.thegospelcoalition.org/article/3-reasons-women-need-good-theology/.

3. Nancy DeMoss Wolgemuth, *A Place of Quiet Rest* (Chicago: Moody, 2002), 174.

Chapter 6 Made to Be He and She

1. Mary Kassian, "Steel Magnolia," The Counsel on Biblical Manhood and Womanhood, April 30, 2009, https://cbmw.org/2009/04/30/steel-magnolia/.

2. Mary Kassian, "The Genesis of Gender," *Preaching Today*, accessed November 28, 2023, https://www.preachingtoday.com/sermons/sermons/2012/february/genesisgender.html.

3. Kassian and Wolgemuth, *True Woman 101*, 85.

4. "Hunting Guide Demographics and Statistics in the US," Zippia, accessed November 28, 2023, https://www.zippia.com/hunting-guide-jobs/demographics/.

5. Kassian and Wolgemuth, *True Woman 101*, 69.

6. David J. Handelsman, Angelica L. Hirschberg, and Stephane Bermon, "Circulating Testosterone as the Hormonal Basis of Sex Differences in Athletic Performance," *Endocrine Reviews* 39, no. 5 (October 2008): 803–29, https://www.ncbi.nlm.nih.gov/pmc/articles/PMC6391653/.

7. Beverly G. Reed and Bruce R. Carr, "The Normal Menstrual Cycle and the Control of Ovulation," updated August 5, 2018, in *Endotext [Internet]*, edited by K. R. Feingold et al. (South Dartmouth, MA: MDText.com, Inc.), https://www.ncbi.nlm.nih.gov/books/NBK279054/.

8. Elisabeth Elliot, *Let Me Be a Woman* (Carol Stream, IL: Tyndale House, 1976), 61.

9. Kassian, "Genesis of Gender."

Chapter 7   God's Radical Design for Marriage and Sex

1. "Does a Wife Have to Submit to Her Husband?," Got Questions, accessed December 22, 2023, https://www.gotquestions.org/wives-submit.html.

2. P.J. Tibayan, "Seeing Jesus on the Stage of Marriage," Desiring God, February 17, 2016, https://www.desiringgod.org/articles/seeing-jesus-on-the-stage-of-marriage.

3. Juli Slattery, "Why Does Sex Matter?," Authentic Intimacy, accessed November 29, 2023, https://www.authenticintimacy.com/why-does-sex-matter/.

Chapter 8   When *She* Decides to Become *He*

1. Pedro L. Gonzales, "Gender Ideology Is a Boon to Big Pharma and Threat to Parental Rights," *New York Post*, August 20, 2021, https://nypost.com/2021/08/20/gender-ideology-a-boon-to-big-pharma-and-threat-to-parental-rights/.

2. Jody L. Herman, Andrew R. Flores, and Kathryn K. O'Neill, "How Many Adults and Youth Identify as Transgender in the United States?," The Williams Institute, June 2022, https://williamsinstitute.law.ucla.edu/publications/trans-adults-united-states/.

3. Abigail Shrier, *Irreversible Damage: The Transgender Craze Seducing Our Daughters* (Washington, DC: Regnery, 2020), 26.

4. Shrier, *Irreversible Damage*, 63.

5. Sam Allberry, "Why Nancy Pearcey Wants You to Love Your Body," The Gospel Coalition, March 7, 2018, https://www.thegospelcoalition.org/article/nancy-pearcey-wants-love-body/.

6. "Gender Dysphoria," Mayo Clinic, accessed June 17, 2024, https://www.mayoclinic.org/diseases-conditions/gender-dysphoria/symptoms-causes/syc-20475255.

7. Andrew T. Walker, "The Transgender Fantasy: What I Wish Every Pastor Knew," Desiring God, July 23, 2022, https://www.desiringgod.org/articles/the-transgender-fantasy.

8. Walker, "Transgender Fantasy."

9. "What Does the Bible Say about the Various Forms of Gender Dysphoria?," Got Questions, accessed November 29, 2023, https://www.gotquestions.org/transsexualism-gender-identity-disorder.html.

10. ArielCAT21, customer review of *The Girl Defined Show*, Apple Podcasts, September 3, 2023, https://podcasts.apple.com/us/podcast/the-girl-defined-show/id1539982603?see-all=reviews.

11. R. Albert Mohler Jr., "The Transgender Revolution and the Death of Truth," Albert Mohler, April 23, 2022, https://albertmohler.com/2022/04/23/the-transgender-revolution-and-the-death-of-truth.

Chapter 9 Falling for the Birth Control Pill

1. "Margaret Sanger (1879–1966)," *The Pill*, PBS, accessed May 13, 2024, https://www.pbs.org/wgbh/americanexperience/features/pill-margaret-sanger-1879-1966/.

2. George Grant, *Killer Angel: A Short Biography of Planned Parenthood's Founder, Margaret Sanger* (Nashville: Highland Books, 2001), 63.

3. Grant, *Killer Angel*, 64.

4. Grant, *Killer Angel*, 79.

5. Jennifer Latson, "What Margaret Sanger Really Said about Eugenics and Race," *TIME*, October 14, 2016, https://time.com/4081760/margaret-sanger-history-eugenics/.

6. Tim Harford, "The Tiny Pill Which Gave Birth to an Economic Revolution," BBC News, May 22, 2017, https://www.bbc.com/news/business-39641856.

7. Harford, "Tiny Pill."

8. Christopher A. Julian, "Median Age at First Marriage, 2021," Bowling Green State University, accessed November 30, 2023, https://www

.bgsu.edu/ncfmr/resources/data/family-profiles/julian-median-age-first
-marriage-2021-fp-22-15.html.

9. Max Roser, "50 Years Ago the Average Woman Had Five Children; Since Then the Number Has Halved," Our World in Data, September 3, 2019, https://ourworldindata.org/global-fertility-has-halved.

10. Louise Tyrer, "Introduction of the Pill and Its Impact," *Contraception* 59, no. 1 (January 1999): 11S–16S, https://doi.org/10.1016/s0010-7824(98)00131-0.

11. Matt Wilstein, "Chelsea Handler: My 3 Abortions Are Why America Needs Roe," Daily Beast, June 27, 2022, https://www.thedailybeast.com/chelsea-handler-says-her-3-abortions-are-why-america-needs-roe-on-jimmy-kimmel-live.

12. Leah Savas, "Unpacking 'My Body, My Choice,'" Crossway, February 20, 2023, https://www.crossway.org/articles/unpacking-my-body-my-choice/.

Chapter 10 Trading In Motherhood for a Career

1. James, *God's Design for Women*, 36–37.

2. James, *God's Design for Women*, 37.

3. Emma Rosenblum, "Later, Baby: Will Freezing Your Eggs Free Your Career?," Bloomberg, April 17, 2014, https://www.bloomberg.com/news/articles/2014-04-17/new-egg-freezing-technology-eases-womens-career-family-angst?.

4. Noah Berlatsky, "Good Day Care Was Once a Top Feminist Priority, and It Should Be Again," *Atlantic*, April 16, 2013, https://www.theatlantic.com/sexes/archive/2013/04/good-day-care-was-once-a-top-feminist-priority-and-it-should-be-again/275027/.

5. Marcia Segelstein, "Inconvenient Truths about Childcare Subvert the Very Best Intentions," *Salvo* 21 (Summer 2012), https://salvomag.com/article/salvo21/daycare-denial.

6. Quoted in Suzanne Venker, "Will America Ever Be Ready for the Truth about Daycare?," *National Review*, February 1, 2012, https://www.nationalreview.com/the-home-front/will-america-ever-be-ready-truth-about-daycare-suzanne-venker/.

Chapter 11 Chasing Beauty at All Costs

1. Jacqueline Howard, "The History of the 'Ideal' Woman and Where That Has Left Us," CNN, March 9, 2018, https://www.cnn.com/2018/03/07/health/body-image-history-of-beauty-explainer-intl/index.html.

2. Howard, "History of the 'Ideal' Woman."

3. Nancy Pearcey, *Love Thy Body: Answering Hard Questions about Life and Sexuality* (Grand Rapids: Baker Books, 2019), 32.

4. Pearcey, *Love Thy Body*, 32.

5. "Should Christians Care about Physical Appearance?," Got Questions, accessed November 30, 2023, https://www.gotquestions.org/physical -appearance.html.

6. Lynn Armstrong, "Biblical Beauty and the Culture Beast," Answers in Genesis, March 8, 2020, https://answersingenesis.org/culture/biblical -beauty-and-culture-beast/.

Chapter 12 I'm a W.O.M.A.N.

1. Rebekah Hargraves, "What Does 'Meek and Quiet' Actually Mean?," Hargraves Home & Hearth, April 8, 2022, https://www.har graveshomeandhearth.com/what-does-meek-and-quiet-actually-mean/.

2. Jessica Brodie, "What Does It Mean to Be a Wife of Noble Character?," Christianity.com, updated November 30, 2023, https://www.chris tianity.com/wiki/bible/what-does-it-mean-to-be-a-wife-of-noble-character .html.

3. "Who Was Ruth in the Bible?," Got Questions, accessed December 30, 2023, https://www.gotquestions.org/life-Ruth.html.

Chapter 13 Living Out Fearless Femininity

1. Kassian, "Recognizing Feminist Thought."

KRISTEN CLARK is married to her best friend, Zack, has three kids, and is the cofounder of Girl Defined Ministries. She is passionate about promoting the message of biblical womanhood through blogging, speaking, mentoring young women, and discipling through her local church. In the end, she's just a fun-lovin' Texas mom who adores all things outdoors and drinks coffee whenever possible.

BETHANY BEAL is head over heels in love with her best friend and husband, David, and is the super-proud mommy of Davey Jr. and Audrey. She is the co-founder of Girl Defined Ministries and is passionate about spreading the truth of biblical womanhood through writing, speaking, and mentoring young women. To her family and close friends, she is simply a tall blonde woman who is obsessed with iced lattes and can't get enough of her sweet babies.

Connect with
Kristen and Bethany

GirlDefined.com

 @GirlDefined @GirlDefined ▶ Girl Defined